THE ART OF
FRIENDLY
CONFRONTATION

THE ART OF
FRIENDLY
CONFRONTATION

CONFLICT RESOLUTION
TO
IMPROVE RELATIONSHIPS

SHIRLEY BRACKETT MATHEY

authorHOUSE®

AuthorHouse™
1663 Liberty Drive
Bloomington, IN 47403
www.authorhouse.com
Phone: 1-800-839-8640

Published by AuthorHouse   05/22/2012

ISBN: 978-1-4685-7989-5 (sc)
ISBN: 978-1-4685-7988-8 (hc)
ISBN: 978-1-4685-7990-1 (e)

Library of Congress Control Number: 2012906541

CONTENTS

PART ONE
WHAT DO YOU THINK AND
FEEL ABOUT CONFLICT?

PART TWO
HOW TO HANDLE CONFLICT

Shirley Brackett Mathey has used these innovative materials for years and produced wonderful results with people. Creative instructor for 26 years at Lincoln Park High School, Shirley developed many innovative materials (slide presentations, flashcards sequences, and group activities).

She wrote her first book on Classroom Activities in 1975. *Students referred to her as the best teacher they ever had.* She worked in advisory roles for school organizations, served as a supervisory teacher for Wayne University, Eastern Michigan and Michigan State Universities. She personally counseled many troubled students, and initiated a weekly classroom peer group counseling sessions. Scores of written appreciations and continuing relationships validate the positive influence upon the lives of young people.

Shirley was active in high school, was leader in 4H club, attended Camp Miniwanca's leadership conference program and received became one of the six chiefs during the 4th year, attended University of Arkansas, University of Michigan and Eastern Michigan Colleges to receive two Masters programs in Family Life Education and Guidance and Counseling.

Shirley is married to her college friend Court Mathey, after her first husband Glenn Brackett died. She has one son Robert Glenn Brackett, Jr. and two grandchildren.

Shirley Brackett

Shirley Brackett Mathey, formerly a popular high school teacher and counselor, was also a professional speaker and seminar leader who presented to business, association and educational groups.

Her credentials include a bachelor's degree in Home Economics from the University of Arkansas, a Master's in Family Life Education from Michigan State University and a Master's in Guidance and Counselor from Eastern Michigan University.

DEDICATION

This book is dedicated to my Daddy, Mr. Carl Heard. His life was an inspiration to me. In the world of wonderful Daddy's, he was the best. I know other people haven't been as fortunate as my sister and I.

My Dad was wise and witty, never dictatorial, allowed me to find my way with very little advice. He was kind, trusting, and did not carry grudges. He enjoyed his family, the outdoors, and storytelling. He was talented, persistent, a hard worker and enjoyed every season of his life. He was very smart and avid reader to find information. The oldest of nine children, his parents died before I was born, but he spoke of them with such adoration I recognized he had been greatly loved. By family trade, he was a sawmill man, but after adversity his life course changed to become a farmer.

Although my Daddy's life was not complicated, Carl Heard was an interesting, honest man of simple accomplishment. At his funeral, at age 85, people came to share wonderful stories about my Daddy. He had obstacles, grief and adjustments to make in life but faced his problems with faith and honor. Could you and I do as well!

ACKNOWLEDGEMENTS

Because of the knowledge I learned in the presence of young people as their Family Living teacher in my years at Lincoln Park High School, I was **driven** to write this book. I enjoyed my students, loved them, worried about them, fussed over them but also got upset with them. However, I finally observed the missing piece of communication skills. Young people don't confront others, well, and as you know, lots of older folks don't do such a hot job either.

There are so many people to give credit in writing a book. My friend, Sue Butram of Cleveland, MS, has been a faithful supporter of my writing skills. BJ Herndon and Ann Marie Dahl, both made valuable corrections. Carol Walters, my Miniwanca friend, made suggestions as she listened to chapter on the way to meetings. Dorothy Lehmkuhl, author of <u>Organizing for the Creative Person</u> of Flat Rock, MI, served as my chief editor and helped keep me focused. Bertie Ryan Synowec of Grosse Ile, MI helped me separate boundaries from confrontation. My sister, Chris Shoemake of Marion, AR has been helpful to me in many ways.

Thank you reader for your perseverance in making differences easier to handle. That's what I hope this book <u>The Art of Friendly Confrontation</u> will do.

PART ONE

WHAT DO YOU THINK AND FEEL ABOUT CONFLICT?

Which Conflict Pattern Do You Use?

FIGHT

"Kill the opponent."

Flight

"Let me get away from this person quickly!"

Chapter 1

TETHERED TOGETHER

CONFLICT IS NORMAL

"*And they lived happily ever after*" is only a fairy tale. We don't live happily ever after. In order to get our way we alternate between sweetness and strife. We want to win! We think, "*I like my way best, and I want you to like it too.*"

What do you think conflict is? Is it people who fight openly or the silent "*if looks could kill?*" Conflict is not always open warfare. Problems often move underground to divert people from the real issues. Some battles are wordless, where the deafening silence controls the partner. Avoidance of open disagreement can deceive us into thinking everything is fine when it's not.

Conflict should be expected. People throughout history have waged strife and wars against each other and it inevitably will continue. We learn conflict strategies and methods from everyone, but how we interpret our emotional experiences is our most important teacher. Because you must consider the choices you must make, conflict is normal, necessary and can be healthy in our decision-making.

Being an individual and unique from others has it's price. When flare ups occur, we struggle internally to decide what to do. Each conflict molds our values, experiences and needs while helping we decide to work with or against others. The more difficulty, the higher our frustration, and the more we feel we need to do something. Although some people seem to enjoy tempers out of hand, most of us don't have the energy to keep it up.

There are benefits from having conflicts, and knowing good things can come from an emotionally draining struggle can aid a person's coping endurance. But in the midst of a hot-tempered argument or long silent siege, it's difficult to remember what they are! It's reasonable to assume bad things can develop, but of course, we know that. The searing white fame in our breast saying "*Kill the opponent,*" occurs when people oppose us on important matters. For others, the message is different. It says, "*Let me get away from this person quickly!*"

ARGUMENTS

⇨   **MONEY**

⇨   **CHILDREN**

⇨   **RELATIVES**

⇨   **RELIGION**

⇨   **POLITICS**

⇨   **TERRITORY**

⇨   **SEX**

CONFLICT IS NECESSARY

Conflict is necessary to assure differing needs are met. Human nature sees things from a selfish point of view. The argument makes sure each side has a say. As infants, the internal weapon is rage: saying "*World! You're not treating me fairly.*" As we mature, anger become more sophisticated and is expressed in gestures, glares, and dialogue. Many people still use rage to handle conflict instead of allowing others to present their side.

There is great value in finishing an argument. The importance of clearing the air and bringing peace was brought home to me years ago when raising my child. There is nothing like child-rearing to rouse your dander. But there is no sweeter apology than the childish kiss from someone who has been reprimanded and climbs on your lap to negotiate peace. When that happens, the balance of equals replaces the gnawing knowledge that someone is pushing your hot buttons. To present peace, we must learn basic coping skills to have fair and effective encounters.

CONFLICT BEGINS EARLY

Conflict begins early. Children disagree over territory, such as sharing a bedroom, owning a toy, or who has the car window. Families argue over pieces of chicken at dinner. Teenagers' territorial fights include "This is my street" or "That is my girl." Office workers have territorial discord over the nicest offices or closets or parking spaces.

Regardless of the issues, people disagree over the same thing: money, children, relatives, religion, politics, territory and sex. The real concerns are the patterns used to handle differences. People approach difficulties in certain learned ways. Our patterns of resolving conflict may not work, or what might have worked when you were younger simply will not in the adult world.

We don't all think alike. Temperament, age, education, cultural upbringing, and gender create differences. I remember a childhood incident where a classmate, day after day, agitated me. I asked, "Maurice, why do you hassle me so much?" Surprisingly, he said, "Because I like you." I couldn't imagine him liking me when I was so frustrated. I moved all over the school bus to avoid him, but he followed me. I remember lashing out at him. As a child, I saw Maurice as the enemy. How I wish I had known how to confront better and become friends.

WHY PROVOKE CONFLICT?

☹ **PLEASURE**

☹ **PEER PRESSURE**

☹ **INSECURITY**

☹ **STATUS**

☹ **BOREDOM**

☹ **ESCAPE**

☹ **REBELLION**

CONFLICT AFFECTS EVERYONE

Why do people provoke conflict? There are dozens of reasons. As a child you witnessed—or have been the victim of—someone's teasing. This may even have appeared to be fun (unless you are the taunted one). Listed below are some reasons why people provoke conflict in others and create dissention.

* Pleasure: to have fun, feel better, or for power.
* Peer Pressure: social alienation, left out of the "in" crowd.
* Insecurity: lack of identity, or low self-esteem.
* Status: to increase image, ego, to ensure fair treatment.
* Boredom: apathy or a need for thrill-seeking experiences.
* Escape: from problems, in school, community.
* Rebellion: against authority—parents, adults, teachers, siblings, and rules, and a desire to prove independence.

HOPELESSNESS

People stay in discouraging relationships for all kinds of reasons. Many stay hoping it will get better. Shame has been defined as not liking who you are, while guilt is not liking what you do. One woman decided "enough" when the abusive husband battered their oldest girl. She had postponed the decision for herself but with child abuse her boldness took over.

Today's increase in battering is a national wake-up call. Physical abuse is the number one cause of injury to women according to a <u>Psychology Today</u> report. One of every two women will be in a battering relationship sometime in her life, and it most likely will begin with pregnancy. Domestic violence affects all, having no barriers of ethnic or socioeconomic class. You are nine times more likely to be killed in a family relationship than on the streets.

Years ago, I saw the despair of Cora's relationship, a retired teacher, who married Jeff in her mature years. Her wealthy father left her with property that she turned over to Jeff to manage. Cora lived in a shabby, run-down home and pitifully explained Jeff's failures. After his death, she discovered Jeff had sold everything and she had nothing. How could this happen to such a sweet, gentle lady? I'm sure Jeff found it easy to manipulate this passive person. Toward the end of her life she said, *"I thought Jeff loved me but now I realize he used me."* Cora abdicated responsibility for herself, because she thought Jeff would provide for her.

POOR
COMMUNICATION

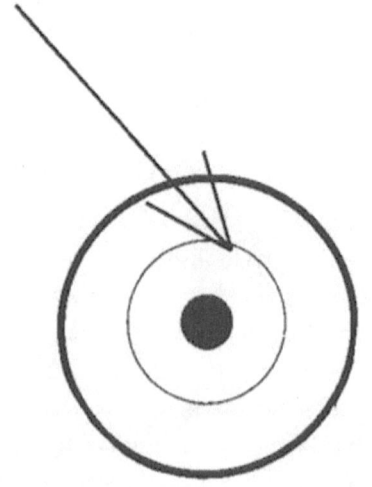

MISSES THE MARK

CONFLICT CAN BE RESOLVED

The bottom line of all conflicts involves lack of communication. Label it avoidance or missed communication, whatever you call it, most people have some difficulty expressing themselves well, particularly when they are upset. We say too much or too little, we say things we regret, or speak superficially instead of what we are really feeling. In conflict, we tend to blame or distort the situation from a personal bias. Being emotionally involved creates a blind spot in the communication.

Effective communication breaks down when:

* People don't always feel free to say what they mean.
* The speaker doesn't say exactly what he/she wants to say.
* Both the speaker and the listener are threatened by loss.
* The listener assumes the speaker knows what to say.
* The same words have different meaning for different people.
* Speakers speak for effect; listeners choose what to hear.
* Listeners have agendas, judge others or become defensive.

CONFLICT CAN HELP YOU GROW

Unsolved problems lead to silence, separation, and despair, but the rewards of resolving conflict are joy, friendship, energy and accomplishment. There is no joy better than regaining a lost friend. Removing an obstacle between people glues the bonds of friendship stronger with each resolved issue. Solving problems empowers partners with a feeling of accomplishment. Fighting and making-up is better than relationships that carry hidden agendas that manipulate.

One study of marital conflict by George R. Back and Peter Wyden concluded that the happiest marriages could *"live with aggression, they learned anger was manageable."* We need to express good feelings of anger. Expressing conflict positively is a decision and can be learned. It's healthy, cleansing, and normal to be frustrated and have a desire to vent; it's a signal to act. Positive anger repairs damaged feelings, and frees you from feeling resentful. Expressing conflict quickly prevents a pile-up of miscommunications, it's full of self, open rather than hidden, and creates a climate to resolve issues. People who demonstrate healthy anger have good opinions of themselves and others and they want to keep it that way.

CONFLICT PRINCIPLES

◎ Behavior triggers behavior,
     both positively and negatively.

◎ Behavior can be categorized
     into four different patterns.

◎ Understanding behavior
     patterns helps you adjust.

◎ Unmet needs can trigger conflict.

◎ Know your behavior pattern.

◎ People can control you by knowing
     your behavior pattern.

◎ Your strongest behavior pattern will
     create a barrier in relationships.

◎ Conflict is essential to growth.

◎ Self esteem comes from recognizing flaws.

Chapter 2

UNDERSTANDING BASIC DIFFERENCES

CONFLICT PRINCIPLES

To deal with conflict effectively, we need to understand behavior principles and the causes of conflict. Recognizing our own contribution to the problem is paramount in conflict resolution. These principles help us look at conflict more objectively.

BEHAVIOR TRIGGERS BEHAVIOR

With maturity, we realize our personal behavior is the one that matters. One customer of a very kind newspaper vendor was always surly, rude and nasty. Another client asked, "How can you stand him?" The vendor replied, "I'm only responsible for my behavior." We respond to others and whatever the situation, people behave either positively or negatively, and this affects us. Behavior can elevate or depress our mood. We are both conscious and unconscious of our responses. There are times we actively seek experiences to change our attitude either positively or negatively.

We work to behave in positive, creative, and uplifting ways but sometimes we are like the little girl in the rhyme "when she was good, she was very, very good, and when she was bad, she was horrid." With good parenting and strong models to discipline our childish behavior, we eventually develop coping strategies.

Thinking people decide to create positive results when they relate with others. It's an act—conceived, believed and practiced. Not setting personal boundaries of how to behave or respond, means you will always react defensively to every situation. Knowing how to improve self respect and relationships even with conflict is the thrust of this The Art of Friendly Confrontation book.

BEHAVIOR STYLES

SANGUINE		CHOLERIC
TALKERS Expressive of Feelings Wants Feelings & Emotions Flexible about Time People Oriented Subjective **FEARS:** Loss of recognition	*Outgoing* *Optimistic* *Outspoken* **LEAD**	**ACHIEVERS** Directive Fast Acting High Risk Takers Verbal Competitors **FEARS:** Being taken advantage of
Witty *Easygoing* *Fun Oriented* **PLAY**		*Decisive* *Organized* *Goal Oriented* **WORK**
AFFILIATORS Inquistive Slow-Acting Low Risk Takers Non-Verbal Cooperators **FEARS:** Loss of security	**ANALYZE** *Introverted* *Pessimistic* *Soft spoken*	**THINKERS** Control of Feelings Want Facts and Figures Precise About Time Task Oriented Objective **FEARS:** Criticism of work
PHLEGMETIC		MELANCHOLY

BEHAVIOR CAN BE CATEGORIZED

As human beings we have a right to be different. Differences over territory (space/right/privileges) is not the most serious of battlegrounds. People even in the same family have serious misunderstandings. We need to treasure our uniqueness, but we need to respect rights and privileges of others. As the author Ruth Strang wrote, *"All people are alike, all people are similar and all people are different."* Our greatest coping skills lie in building bridges to harmonize with others, to value and embrace their differences.

People think differently about the same experience. In 400 B.C., Hippocrates, known as the father of medicine, observed four different behaviors. "Assuming they had a bodily cause, he used the body moistures to name the behaviors: the blood, he called Sanguine for a subjective, cheerful, talkative, expressive person. The bile, he labeled, he labeled Choleric, for the fast acting, verbal and short tempered, driven high risk takers. The phlegm, he named Phlegmatic for a slower moving, nonverbal amiable low risk taking individual, who stay calm and collected under pressure. Melancholy, uses melas, a Greek work for black, and chole for analytical, time conscious, critical, deep thinking or gifted geniuses." (From Florence Littauer, <u>Personality Tree</u>)

UNDERSTANDING TEMPERAMENTS HELPS YOU ADJUST

Just as there are four winds, people behave consistently in the four behaviors, which we now call temperaments. In the Expressive temperament people behave as friendly, enthusiastic, stimulating and sometimes manipulative. In the Driven category, behaviors are determined, dominating, demanding and pushy. Amiable people are more likely to be softhearted, persistent, accepting and complying. The Analytical temperament will be industrious, exacting, critical and serious. To simplify, some people act more out-going while others are more passive, some are cooperative while others are task oriented.

We have all the temperaments, but, we choose to believe we have only one or two of them. The descriptions in the visual will help you identify categories of human behavior. People normally operate from one quadrant. Recognizing our strengths or weaknesses helps adjust our behavior. Examine the characteristics of each category to appreciate people's differences. You can manage conflict better when you recognize the four behavior patterns of those people you encounter.

SELF
ACTUALIZATION

SELF ESTEEM
TO FEEL IMPORTANT

TO BELONG
TO GIVE AND
TO RECEIVE LOVE

SAFETY & SECURITY

(FEAR OF LOSS - FAILURE - PUNISHMENT- PAIN)

PHYSICAL NEEDS
(AIR- WATER - FOOD - SHELTER - SLEEP)

CONFLICT CAN BE TRIGGERED BY UNMET NEEDS

The core of a person is represented by needs. When someone blocks our getting our needs met, we project ourselves accordingly.

Every conflict deals with one of these core needs. Abraham Maslow prioritized human needs in life continuing hierarchy. The person with all needs met and still developing his potential, he called self actualized. Maslow's human needs are: **physical needs, safety, to be loved, to belong, self esteem and feeling important, and finally self actualized**.

We have physical needs. These include water, food, clothing, shelter, sleep, activities, and biological needs. Many of our routine activities can lead to irritability and quarrels when needs are not net. When someone is tired or hungry, one cannot function well. To illustrate, a women's need for being organized and having all chores finished, may differs from her spouse's. When to start and return from shopping trips all create lively discussions.

We have safety needs. These include freedom from loss, fear, pain, failure, punishment and threats. Security and procedures for safety can create discord. Trips back to check and recheck the house is locked, the stove is off, and the iron disconnected do not set well with everyone. My passive Dad, tired of Mother's anxious routine, announced as they left on one trip, "Your medicine and iron are in the trunk of the car."

The need to give and receive love affects our ability to cope, since it connects us to all our relationships. Being loved is essential to the give and take process so necessary in healthy conflict. Lack of love teaches us not to trust, to love conditionally, to deceive and manipulate others, and creates fearful responses when adversity strikes. Unloved people tend to have poor coping skills. The need to belong translates into thinking we want people to be like us and are insulted when we realize they aren't. I assumed one friend and I had the same religious interpretation of an issue. We did think the same at all! Expectations create conflict in relationships.

We need to feel important. We struggle to find a life worth living. As Peggy Lee's song inquires. "Is that all there is?" We yearn to be different from our friends and relatives; our activities, clothing, homes, religions and work help us feel noble, worthy and important. New experiences add perspective and depth to our lives but also offer us insight, meaning and prestige.

MASLOW'S
VALUES CONTRASTED

MANIPULATORS

Deception
Phoniness
Betrayal
Conniving

Boredom
Apathetic
Monotonous
Dullness

Control
Closed
Dominating

Cynicism
Distrust
Sarcasm

ACTUALIZORS

Honesty
Transparency
Geniuneness
Authenticity

Awareness
Responsiveness
Aliveness
Interested

Freedom
Spontaneity
Generosity

Trust
Faith
Belief

Self Actualization is using our talents to go beyond ourselves to conquer adversity and make a difference in the world about us. Using our inborn disposition from a position of strength, we become a larger person and make this world a better place. Self actualizors take the world seriously and themselves lightly. They have a well developed philosophy and could be called "a character," because they are unforgettably unique.

According to Abraham Maslow, the self actualized person lives in four positive attitudes: honesty, awareness, freedom and trust. He appreciates his own talents. He become congruent by communicating the same messages he feels, thus is "true to himself." By contrast, manipulators are fearful and never quite believe they are okay. They operate negatively and selfishly using deception, control, boredom, and cynicism to encounter others.

Probably the words most descriptive of people are the terms positive and negative. These words summarize the value system many families teach without realizing it. My Dad taught through his life experience to make your word your bond with people. Although not formally educated, he was an informed as Dr. Maslow about the positive values that make a difference in life.

CONFLICT CAN BE PART OF THE GROWTH PROCESS

The cycle of giving and receiving in relationship works with positive response in people; this actualized process works toward all peoples' good. Manipulators work with a negative push and take attitude; a negative process that uses deception.

The actualizor appreciates his uniqueness, and operates from a position of worth to those around him. The manipulator see others as the enemy, the world as a battleground and uses the negative attitudes of deception, unawareness, control, and cynicism to control his world. "A manipulator is a person who exploits, uses, or controls himself and others as 'things' in self defeating ways," says Everett Shostrum in his book, Man The Manipulator.

On the next page you will find Shostrum's examples of people who, using their inner strengths, exhibited the self actualized characteristics. The potential manipulating behavior is also shown.

Respecter—Gandhi, a man of non violence who deeply respected those with whom he dealt. **Leader**—Churchill exemplified the greatest leadership to the English people during World War II. **Assertor**—Lincoln was not hostile or dominating during his debates, and demonstrated his lack of vindictiveness during the Civil War.

MANIPULATOR OR

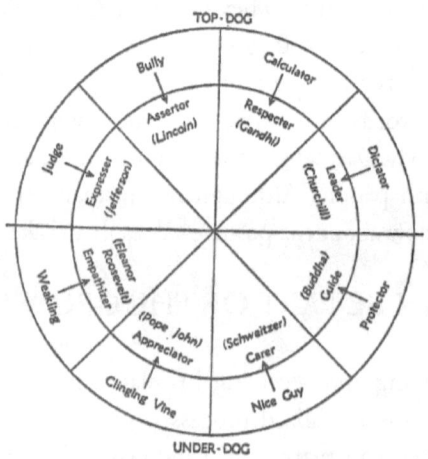

SELF ACTUALIZOR

Expresser—Jefferson expressed tolerance and nonjudgment of others in this writings. **Appreciator**—Pope John XXIII was non-judgmental, people didn't have to think the same as he. **Empathizer**—Eleanor Roosevelt listened to the needs of the underdeveloped nations and accepted the human tendency to err. **Carer**—Albert Schweitzer served the African people with deep devotion and dedication to them. **Guide**—Buddha did not protect or teach others, rather he helped each person find his way.

Knowing temperaments will produce more harmonious relationships.

STRONG BEHAVIOR PATTERNS CAN CREATE BARRIERS

Through the process of growing up, we adjusted and applied new coping skills. However, we use certain behaviors over and over and, when it becomes comfortable, individuals begin to believe: "**That's the way I am.**" People rely on familiar patterns without flexing their behavior muscles.

A pattern of behavior comfortable to you becomes observable to others. When two different needs appear, we desire to make our point. Others will use your behavior pattern against you, thus creating conflict.

In an adult quilting class, Sophia became indignant when I asked her if her children helped her financially. "*No, I don't want any help from them.*" Since she was working on quilts for gifts to give her twelve children, I reminded her of the joy she received from her giving. I asked her how she would feel if her children told her they didn't want her to give anymore. This surprised her, she had never thought about robbing her children of the greatest strength she had; that of giving. The next weekend her furnace blew up, and a new furnace was installed with the children sharing the cost.

KNOW YOUR BEHAVIOR PATTERN

People have to be confronted with something big to make a behavior change. Unchallenged, we drift, wander or stagnate into behaviors and may feel unloved. An example of drifting came from my first year in marriage. I stayed in my robe on the weekends until late in the afternoon. My husband came from a family where the females came dressed to the breakfast table. My husband said, "Would you please try getting dressed early in the morning and see how it makes you feel?" I accomplished more, and wasn't embarrassed when someone came to the door.

BEHAVIOR STYLES

OUTGOING

COOPERATIVE

EXPRESSIVE
Friendly
Enthusiastic
Stimulating
Manipulative

DRIVEN
Determined
Dominating
Demanding
Pushy

TASK ORIENTED

AMIABLE
Soft Hearted
Persistent
Accepting
Complying

ANALYTICAL
Industrious
Exacting
Critical
Serious

PASSIVE

When I first recognized my strong expressive temperament, it confirmed what I always knew about myself. My undeveloped area was the analytical category, the direct opposite of my strength. I had difficulty appreciating analytical people who got a kick out of details! When an analytical person pointed out my lack of attention to detail, I bristled! I now recognize their strengths are my weakness, and visa versa: we are each other's teacher. Not always easy, but I appreciate differences now.

OTHER PEOPLE KNOW YOUR BEHAVIOR PATTERN

As the bright age of 18, Elaine determined that if she took a job downtown, she would spend her money. The other option was to baby-sit for a family nearby, and iron for me. Every week she would tell me the state of her relationship with her fiancé, Bob. Yet, as time went on, some problems developed in the relationship. Bob spent all his money. One October day, she came in very upset. Bob bought a bowling ball but had nothing saved. The wedding was on hold.

Sitting down with her at the table I said, "I think Bob is dependent on you and therefore he doesn't have to save." In fact, my secret name for you is "Economical Elaine." But, if you want him to save, you must switch roles and start enjoying your money. Why don't we call you "Frivolous Elaine" instead of "Economical Elaine."

After thinking it over, Elaine realized how predictable she had become. She had been scraping lipstick with a hairpin and wearing shoes, coats and clothes purchased in high school. She badly needed a hair cut, makeup and new shoes; she decided to change her image. She took Bob on spending sprees to convince him she was really spending money. One night, she exclaimed "Stop, I must go in that drug store." He waited while she stayed a long time. Coming out of the drugstore, she bragged she had purchased her first false fingernails. Bob, observing this behavior, became alarmed. They discussed money seriously and he saved enough money for an August wedding.

LIFE SCRIPTS

I Win   —   You Win

I Win   —   You Lose

I Lose   —   You Win

I Lose   —   You Lose

SELF ESTEEM AND CONFLICT

Eric Berne's book, <u>Games People Play</u>, gives an analytical description of life scripts. These interpret how our needs have been fulfilled. Based on the psychological ego states, Berne labeled Parent, Adult, Child, he described how we live scripts based on our belief systems. These life scripts summarize feelings about self and others. The simple code reads:

LIFE SCRIPT	RELATIONSHIP MEANING
I'm O.K. You're O.K.	Healthy, fulfilling and successful
I'm O.K. You're not O.K.	Blaming, I'm not at fault.
I'm not O.K. You're O.K.	Defensive, loser, druggie
I'm not O.K. You're not O.K.	I'm crazy. You're crazy.

Berne defined the meaning behind the scripts as the ability to give and receive love, the cycle he called "the unit of human recognition." He stated, "Human survival depends on accumulating strokes; even negative strokes will suffice if no positive ones are available." In a positive environment, a surplus of recognition is given. Our life script is observable through our conflict behavior.

Self esteem is based on positive relationships with others. However, we all know some people who have socially unacceptable behaviors and usually wind up with poor self esteem. Dennis Waitley, author and speaker, aptly describes "the Assassin and Terrorist; who hurt others and take victims, the Abuser, who is saying *"I'll show you, Bullies, who get their kicks form seeing others squirm and the Cheat, who steals value from everyone."*

Socially accepted behaviors have varying amounts of self esteem such as "the Braggart," who says arrogantly, "Look what I did." The Clown plays to the audience for laughs, while the Materialistic person deals with others competively. The Achiever wants respect and recognition for contributions, while the Altruistic, seeks an inner feeling of esteem by giving it to others."

Understanding basic behaviors may be helpful in recognizing people with high self esteem. Different people use different words to describe healthy personalities but they have much of the same meaning. Whether we use Maslow's terminology, Denis Waitley's or Eric Berne's, we know how some people like themselves and others don't. The ability to like yourself helps bridge the path to meet others when differences arise. Thinking people know the secret to developing self esteem: it comes from giving it to someone else.

THE INFLATED EGO

"I'M RIGHT YOU'RE WRONG"

Chapter 3

EGO—THE NEED TO FEEL IMPORTANT

DEFENSIVENESS

The ego is an emotional protection from changes demanded by the outside world. Some people, desirous of keeping the status quo, are defensive about change, and have a great need to stay where they are. They want to be right, avoid being wrong, or corrected. Our ego defenses may become too strong to connect with others. Certain people value their opinion more than others and have a "Big I, little you" attitude. To change our mind requires effort.

The ego defenses are really fences keeping ourselves intact. It's easy to understand defensiveness as the invisible bubble we use to keep others away. It protects us from others when they get too close, we may attack. Sometimes we protect ourselves correctly, but at times we act inappropriately. We want others to love us, but knowing they can hurt us, we attack in certain ways: blaming, criticism, dependency, and rage.

LEARNED PATTERNS OF BEHAVIOR

Look at your upbringing to recognize your temperament style and determine how it relates to your ego, thus your self esteem. While it is good to be passive, learning to be adjustable with your temper is a valuable asset. Being passive doesn't inform others you are upset. When people lose control, the raging energy becomes a surprise—overwhelming, even embarrassing to those it concerns.

People with strong egos fail to admit they make mistakes. Since mistakes are normal in life, the person who rejects making mistakes has difficult apologizing, and forgiving others who make mistakes.

PROBLEM SOLVING IS SIMPLE

AGREES

1) What is the problem?

BRAINSTORMS

2) What can we do?

EVALUATES

3) Which solution is best?

DECIDES

4) Who does what, when?

ARGUMENTS ARE DIFFICULT

They Problem Solve Backwards

They First Decide

WHO—DOES WHAT—WHEN

THE IMPORTANCE OF REACHING BOTTOM

An alcoholic must admit *"I have a problem with alcohol,"* and people with relationship problems eventually must confront, *"I have a problem with your behavior." Feeling resentment doesn't solve the problem; being angry doesn't work; games and silence won't make it go away. You are part of the problem and part of the solution."* As James Baldwin stated, *"Confrontation doesn't always bring a solution, but until you confront the problem there will be no solution."*

Dale Carnegie's book, How To Win Friends and Influence People, reminded us to see things from the other person's vantage point. The ultimate low is admitting you are part of the problem; and someone else has a point worth understanding.

Human nature blames others for things gone awry instead of taking responsibility for personal actions. When listening to people complain, we hear the recurring blaming refrain, "it's their fault, not mine." The principle, *"I am responsible for my thinking, my feelings and my behavior,"* corrects the blaming syndrome. The devil doesn't make you do it. *"You made you do it!"* President Truman said it well with a desk sign: *"The buck stops here."*

THE EGO AND DECISION MAKING

Since our ego wants us to hold on to what we have, it's an internal tug of war to move in a new direction. And yet no decision becomes a decision. Some individuals don't make decisions, they blame, postpone, abdicate responsibilities, or rely on others to make choices. A person who can make decisions (a clean cut heals better than a ragged tear) recognizes in conflict the choices may not be pretty but a choice will be the better of the two evils.

The need to prove we are right overwhelms our ability to think rationally. The willingness to say, "I could be wrong" is a key to cooperative decision making. Not always controlling what is going to happen in a situation invites others to contribute. Saying you could be wrong opens the door for others to admit error.

Problem solving involves 1) **agreeing:** What is the problem? People who can agree on the problem continue to 2) **brainstorm:** What can we do about it? Then they can 3) **evaluate:** Which solution is best. Lastly they 4) **decide:** Who does what when. Amusingly, many people do this process exactly backwards. After the argument they eventually have to go back to discover what is the problem! Instead of *"Ready, Aim, Fire, it's "Fire, Aim, Ready!"*

THE RIGHT
QUESTION
TO ASK

"How can I make this

bad thing good?"

CONTINUING TO LEARN

An eighteen year old young lady seated by an elderly white haired gentleman asked: "What do you do by profession?" The elderly man state "*I devote myself to the study of physics.*" The woman replied, "*You mean you actually study physics at your age*" *Why I finished my studies a year ago.*" This true story of Albert Einstein illustrates someone who hadn't come to understand that one must always continue learn. People with poor coping skills assume that they have already mastered them when they have only begun.

Because the ego is resistant to change, in crisis situations we reuse behavior that once got results. Continuing to learn helps us look adversity straight in the eye and accept whatever happens. The pathway we choose decides if we will be better or worse. We can grow or to hold on to the pain. Since misfortune greets the human race in different times and forms in life, we can choose each experience as a building block or an obstacle to avoid. "*Rarely does creative endurance, or courage, become possible without the introduction of adversity,*" as Gail Sheehy said in her book, Pathfinders.

THE RIGHT QUESTION TO ASK

How do you face adversity? When you have a major set-back in your life, what can you do? 1) You can curse because life has given you this obstacle, but people will soon tire of hearing you complain. 2) You can grit your teeth and endure, but, to follow through with that much pent up anger is exhausting and creates bitterness. 3) When up you let go and accept it; tolerate it, learn from it, you will adjust. Letting go of the hurt allows the experience to be your teacher.

There is an adage about difficult time: "All you have to do is adjust." This philosophy has much of the understanding needed in life to survive successfully. There are few absolutes in the world. The only thing we can depend on is change. Many times we can change our attitude when we can't change our physical surroundings. It's the attitudes of inflexibility that creates much of the misery in the world.

When adversity happens there may be no best answers, but **are you asking the right question**? "How can this bad thing be happening to me?" This question will keep you stuck and will delay a solution. "How can I make this bad thing good?" This questioning attitude stretches your thinking to find a positive answer.

ANGER IS

ENERGY

ESCALATING

A TOOL

A HABIT

A DECISION

AN ASSET

TRANSITORY

COMMUNICATION

Chapter 4

ANGER—THE NEED TO SEPARATE

ANGER IS ENERGY

Conflict is neither good nor bad, it's a force for making changes when presented with differences. A necessary tool to protect us in conflict, anger produces amazing energy. It fuels the body, fractures your peace of mind and zaps your ability to concentrate.

An intolerable situation mobilizes our inner resources so that we can deal with injustices around us. Throughout history, people outraged by various obstacles used their anger constructively. Being angry can be one of your greater assets. Saying "I'm not going to take it anymore," is fine but it's better to identify how to make it better for everyone.

Anger's energy must be disciplined or we will destroy all in it's pathway. It can be harnessed for our good as well as for the good of others. In California, a father grieving over his daughter's death, organized the petition drive, "Three Strikes and You're Out." A mother, enraged over a drunk driver who killed her child, organized MADD. Elizabeth Taylor, compassionate and enraged about family and friends dying, organized a massive AIDS effort.

LEVELS OF ANGER

The two patterns of expressing anger, fight and flight, operate like a continuum. People fight in many ways, some are direct and loud while other fight mean and dirty and sneaky. Some people are may cry, or be quiet and moody.

Researchers estimate two-thirds of our personal communication is wordless; a smile, a taunt jaw, a stern look, a clenched fist. The gestures tell others your mood, feelings and whether you are approachable. These wordless communications can be venomously angry.

Angry can destroy the positive forces previously operating. Angry feelings are transitory; they remain between 10 to 45 seconds. When people think about their hurt feelings, the feelings then become rehearsed, demonstrated and phony. (Have you ever frowned for days to prove to someone how mad you were?)

Three Stages Of
ANGER

- **VERBALIZED**

- **DEMONSTRATED**

- **DELAYED**

VERBALIZED ANGER

Verbalized anger is the beginning level of sharing real feelings of hurt where others can understand your suffering and come to your aid. Verbalized anger identifies and reports the tiny hurt feelings that help people stay connected. It is important to express feelings of anger appropriately; to the right person, at the right time, in the right place, to the degree of the wrong; and lastly, to discuss feelings about the incident.

You can't assume people know when your feelings get hurt, you must tell them immediately, it's the only way for them to have new information. People maintain high self esteem when they share feelings appropriately and lost it when they don't. People in deep depression have a "frozen rage" concerning unexpressed anger.

DEMONSTRATED ANGER

People who demonstrate anger throw things, slam doors, push others around or scream obscenities. A physical outburst of energy is an example of over learned expression of anger. When a person angers quickly and demonstrates it every time, people respond with insincere and temporary changes.

We submit to angry people at first because they won't let us continue behavior as usual. We deal with them! People eventually become numb with repeated demands. Acting "I'm mad at you" creates a response of "So what!" The normal response to someone who blows their stack too often is "Click, here they go again!"

This stage of anger can become a habit. We often witness a behavior style while growing up and as an adult, we assume the same behavior stance. It's like a recipe. The danger is with adult power we take on the patterns learned without questioning them.

DELAYED ANGER

Anger is source of frustration, it upsets us; we lose our confidence and peace of mind. The quiet passive person delays handling uncomfortable situations and controls their behavior when others are venting. Sometimes an intolerable condition continues until civility doesn't work. When the delayed anger finally is released, it's out of control, explosive and violent.

Anger
must be
SELF
DISCIPLINED

Delayed, buried anger becomes an act of revenge saying, "I'm not going to take it anymore!" This abnormal range of behavior is energy gone awry and must go somewhere. Without the practice of sharing anger in early stages, delayed anger comes out too strong. The man who brings his gun to work to kill his fellow workers may have endured a traumatic experience. People comment later, he "didn't give anyone any trouble," or "never seemed unhappy."

People who control feelings and believe and act with propriety must identify and announce feelings and believe and act with propriety must identify and account for feelings quickly. It's the body's safety valve. When rape, robbery and rampage are commonplace, using intuitive feelings could save our life. Women are encouraged to scream insults at an attacker before possession of their body, car or home, but timidity gets in the way.

ANGER ENTRENCHED

In the book, <u>Anger Kills</u>, Redford and Virginia Williams describe how habitual anger produces a continuing physical disruption to the body. Anxiety creates and pours adrenaline into the system, giving the person more power than they normally have. This chemical is harmful in large amounts and stresses the system until, with time a major weakness in the body finally ruptures. Anger becomes perpetuating: the expression given mildly, the more angry a person becomes. Anger can become a habit.

The relationship problems with habitually angry people are observable. The face, mannerism and conversation assume a fighting stance. Their anger limits their cooperation since correction cannot be tolerated. They have few friends, therefore receive little honest feedback from others.

The principle of momentum works in many areas of life: the snowballing effect says once you turn you anger on, it continues and intensifies. Anger escalates. Research reports the higher the verbal aggression, the more physical aggression will occur. The question is: What do you want to continue? Obviously, anger must be self disciplined! Others controlled it temporarily when we were young but the ultimate challenge is recognizing we are responsible for our anger, not our parents, the schools, the police nor society at large.

"I'M MAD"
Is TOO Global

sad

hurt   insulted

put upon embarrassed

frustrated   irritated

livid   depressed

upset

Say Specific Feelings
IMMEDIATELY

GENDER ANGER

Society has programmed specific gender anger responses. Men hide their emotions but use physical aggression in anger, whereas women share feelings and use less physical contact. There are exceptions; some passive men become "teddy bears," and some females display "tiger" behavior. Dr. Theodore Isaac Rubin states, "It's the repression of anger, not it's expression, that's the most dangerous." Boys become aggressive while girls become submissive; "it's not ladylike to show your anger." This difference creates men who become more abusive. The public is more aware that black eye, bruises, and cracked bones come from the hands of loved ones.

OVERCOMING INHIBITIONS

Anger is not just an emotion, it's a response to fear, particularly fear of loss of something you love. A great chasm lies between feeling angry and thinking angry. Feeling angry is a normal built-in protection lasting only a very few seconds. It's an assault; someone destroyed our calm. True anger is first a hurt; rejection, resentment, or even being taken for granted. Thinking about being angry is defining how to behave: where coping strategies are made and carried out. Have you ever said to yourself "I'll show them?" Coping has many faces; we choose to avoid people, change the subject, joke about it, apologize, threaten, withdraw, or perhaps see the person's point of view.

When people are angry they may use the words, "I'm mad." However, saying "I'm mad," is too large, too global, yet too indirect for other to identity with your pain. Say specifically what you feel. Showing anger is threatening, while saying nothing hides the hurt and intensifies the pain. People connect easier by identifying the specific hurt. The old cliché "do the thing you fear and the death of the fear is certain" applies here. Problem solving can't start until people's feelings have been identified and shared. This creates calmness so people can be open to problem solving. After you learn to discuss feelings, problem solving becomes easier.

People must overcome inhibitions to make a simple statement of pain. You can't assume the other person knows what you need emotionally until you tell them. Stay neutral to your partner's insensitivity, hostility and rejection when delivering your message of pain. Persistence, which doesn't give up on either of you, is a necessary trait of working through inhibitions when you decide to tell others how you feel.

PURPOSE OF
POWER

- ## CONTROL

- ## RESTRAIN

- ## DESTROY

Chapter 5

POWER STRUGGLE—
THE NEED TO CONQUER

WHERE POWER BEGINS

People love power. In fact, when you think of card games or competive sport, the sweet final retorts of "Gotcha" or "We won!" tell only part of the story. The whole purpose of the game is to exhibit power. Could game skills contribute to the competitiveness for power in the family, office and school?

Many factors determine the use of power besides human nature: size, age, competition, culture. Some 2 year old children grab a toy, claiming, "It's Mine." This seems to extend to the dating years when they "own" their sweethearts, as well. Controlling others contributes to unhappiness.

Women and children were once considered "chattel," the goods, property and wealth of the men who owned them. Now, some powerful women display the precious inequities formerly attributed to men. The women's movement raised the curtain for women to vote, to learn, earn and keep their money.

PURPOSE OF POWER

The purpose of power is to control, restrain and destroy. Appropriate use of power is healthy, necessary and productive. We are seeing mounting evidence where the inappropriate use of power produces violence in family. You are far more likely to be abused, hurt, maimed or murdered by a family member than on the street.

Power eventually become an issue of selfishness. Nature has a built-in imprint that says *I want what I want when I want it.* Without restraints, parental training, and learning to share, we think we are God, and what we think, say, or do is omnipotent. That is, until someone sets us straight!

IF YOU DON'T
LEARN
THIS LESSON
NOW

THE NEXT ONE
WILL BE

MORE

DIFFICULT

Power begins when we know we have won. We crave it because it feels so good! Power, an aphrodisiac of the head, is not emotion but cares for detached things, becomes cool and calculated, it's stimulates the feeling of accomplishment, and creates a desire for more control. Power corrupts and eventually destroys most people. When people decide to be free from restraint from anyone or anything, with time and practice they can force others to yield to them even against their will. Then only a stronger force can bring them back within the bounds of society again.

PAINFUL LESSONS TEACH

Life is simply a series of lessons designed to help us mature so we can relate more meaningfully with others, When you don't learn the lessons life teaches the first time, the next time around they will be harder. It doesn't matter when or from where the experience come, painful lessons will instruct. I wanted to quit school when kids called me a bad name, but my mother said, "You may be called bad names all your life, that doesn't mean you quit what you are doing." I wanted to quit liking boys when Jimmy never told me why he broke up with me. I wanted to quit college when I got a "D" on my Chemistry test. When I had an overbearing supervisor I realized, my mother was right; you can't quit when things are painful.

Power without love is ruthless and even love with some authority is helpless. Power interferes with love and therefore rejects real relationships. Relationships with a person who uses power creates pain for the non-powerful partner. At first the non-powerful partner works to avoid pain. When pain becomes the teacher, the person has a choice: does he or she use **power or authority** in retaliation?

WHERE AUTHORITY BEGINS

The opposite of power is authority. Authority persuades others to recognizes that what you ask is legitimate and right. Authority means you are the creator of a situation involving respect, legality and have consideration for others. Power deals with intimidation, and dominance over others. We realize Mother Teresa had great authority, but little or no power. The world would lead us to believe that power is better than authority, but people like Mother Teresa teach us differently. Authority and appropriate leadership roles are imperative for good relationships. The author Max Weber wrote about cities, "When the authority decreases, power increases," but this is personal as well.

"The person who loves the least has the most power.

The person who loves the most has the least power."
Williard Waller

PRINCIPLE OF LEAST INTEREST

In the thirties, Willard Waller penned the Principle of Least Interest: "*The person who loves the least has the most power—the person who loves the most has the least power.*" From love stories told and retold is this dominating theme. The person who loves the most gives more to keep the relationship going. The selfish partner intuitively seizes the moment by enticing the loved one to meet his needs, desires or demands. The beginning of a power struggle starts with knowing someone will do anything for you. People can control you if they know your behavior pattern. Your strongest behavior pattern overused will create a barrier in a relationship. Love gets in the way. Therefore the Principle of Least Interest becomes a basic concept of the power struggle.

BEING VICTIMIZED

Evie, married at fourteen to an older fellow, was the mother of six children before she was twenty four. Because she was subservient, her husband found she would accept any crumbs he would offer. While he drank and pursued other women, she came to a realization that much of her pain came from loving him too much. If she was to be treated with respect, she simply became an authority in her life. She stopped letting him know she loved him until she had security and respect.

Evie concluded correctly that life would not change until she changed it. That is the essence of coping; to take authority into our own hands and make something useful of it. Evie lived through and conquered her pain without a formal education, and yet, she changed her life positively.

In a power struggle, where loving someone can get in the way, does that mean love is to be ignored? On the contrary: it's a question of self-esteem. Do you love yourself enough to demand respect? A person with high self esteem encourages respect for self, their partner, and the relationship; people with low esteem will settle for survival.

ROLE'S

PLACEMENT

**Are you Playing a
TOP DOG or UNDER DOG Role**

POWER

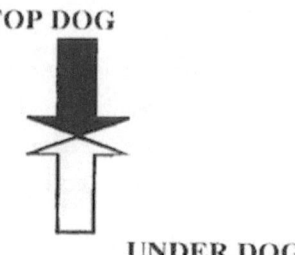

TOP DOG

UNDER DOG

REVERSAL

**UNDER DOG
ASSUMES
TOP DOG
ROLE**

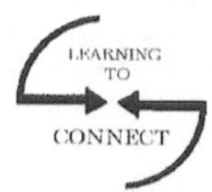

LEARNING
TO

CONNECT

ROLE PLACEMENT

In every relationship there is one person who loves more. Individuals in a relationship will assume the roles of "Top-Dog" and "Under Dog." As I listened to young people's problems, I heard the story of relationship control often repeated and recognized it as a pattern of pretty normal behavior.

As a teacher, it seemed appropriate to share my courtship story with my students. In the first six months of courtship my future husband pursued me until I was smitten. After a verbal commitment of love, it was obvious to everyone that I cared. A break-up occurred when I observed a gradual change in my sweetie, and began feeling taken for granted. Later, we made up and I restored the pattern saying "I love you." But "being taken for granted" escalated and my pain intensified when my threats fell on deaf ears. My parents, roommate, and friends warned me the relationship was one sided. Eventually I quit taking total responsibility for the relationship, I quit tending and nurturing the relationship; I even refused to write or phone, I also decided that if there was a relationship, it would have to come from him. My guard was up; I determined I was going to be treated with courtesy.

When I <u>let go </u>of the relationship, my eyes opened to others and in less than a week, I was dating. I would not be an "Under-Dog" any more. Three months went by before an apology came. I was curt on the phone but inside I felt relieved that my "letting go" behavior had stabilized our roles. Relationships must come from both people and I refused to do more than my share. Later, with a confession and apology of the mistakes made, we made plans for a wedding.

ROLE POWER

When poor behavior becomes entrenched the situation becomes tense. When one dominates, the other experiences powerlessness. In that five year romance, I learned love relationships need some mystery. I recognized my strong behavior pattern was overused and created a barrier in our relationship. To reassure someone that you love them without having an equal commitment, as I did, allows them to manipulate you. You don't know where you stand and can be mistreated. What I felt was confusion, because I heard his words but the behavior did not match. In the under-dog position, one tries to please, even in great pain.

GIVING
&
RECEIVING

BALANCES THE
YING-YANG

ROLE REVERSAL

The power struggle reverses when the Under-Dog stops doing their share of the relationship tending. The stressed "Under-Dog" roles works too hard for justice, but nothing will happen until the roles are balanced. When you quit doing everything, will they return to mend fences? Years ago, a popular poster with a seagull in the background stated "If you love someone, let them go free, if they don't come back, it never was."

Role reversal works because unsatisfied needs motivate. When a person has an increase in pain, they lose their sense of control. When the Under-Dog relaxes, this switches the balance and changes the relationship. The partner will miss the caretaking, it frees the inertia for them to work again to get things back to normal. The role change is working when the previous dominating person, now an Under-Dog comes back to renotigate the relationship. We fear the relationship will not survive the testing. The real danger isn't that they won't come back, but when they do will they resume the old behaviors that were uncomfortable and habit-forming? If they never come back, that's good news; you didn't have a relationship after all! The intensity and length of the break-up are important to help establish new rules of treatment.

Forgiveness must set new boundaries for the relationship to continue growing in the right direction.

GIVING AND RECEIVING

In looking at relationships as a cycle of giving and receiving, the proverb that giving is more blessed than receiving is a principle of truth not to be overlooked. We find joy in giving to those we love. The problem occurs when you give and give and the reciprocal part of giving gets stifled. When you do it all, you rob the other person of doing for you. The Under-Dog works hard while the Top-Dog works very little. The ying-yang isn't flowing, it's unbalanced. The Chinese symbol representing movement is stuck.

Beautiful relationships stabilize themselves into a balance of the 50/50 ratio. One person assumes the Top-Dog role in some areas of life and in other areas assumes the Under-Dog role. This giving and receiving balances the power. People relax when giving and receiving becomes a ying-yang: the balanced to-and-fro distribution of power feels comfortable.

PART TWO

HOW TO HANDLE CONFLICT

SELF DISCLOSURE

SPEAK FOR YOURSELF
Use I, Me, My or Mine

SAY WHAT YOU FEEL
Stay in the present

SAY WHAT YOU THINK

SAY WHAT YOU WANT

SAY WHAT YOU WILL DO

Chapter 6

THE COPING SKILLS— SELF DISCLOSURE AND LISTENING

SELF DISCLOSURE

Accepting responsibility for ourselves is the ultimate maturity. It's what separates children from adults. Maturity admits the obvious, good and bad, and simply tells the truth about ourselves. Edmund Burks said, "All that is necessary for the forces of evil to win in the world is for enough good men to do nothing." The forces of evil will win when we do not first choose honesty in ourselves.

Self disclosure informs others who we are. Like a two edged sword, taking responsibility for ourselves and with others cuts to the heart of every matter. Surprisingly, when you allow others to see your weaknesses, the more people will appreciate, respect and support you. People who portray themselves as never making mistakes, defeat genuineness in relationships. The paradox of telling on yourself is produces beauty and great magnetism. We are afraid of rejection. In fact when you reveal things about yourself, people will open up and tell on themselves.

Self disclosure keeps a relationship in the present. Sharing feelings on a continuing basis is the essence of a growing friendship, hidden feelings seep out in indirect ways. Expressed feelings are the groundwork for keeping relationships alive and growing. This congruency of feelings, expressing on the outside when you feel on the inside is the essence of vulnerability.

CENTERED FEELINGS

Being centered comes from a core of self-love, rather that working to please the world at large. Centered feelings create many positive results such as:
* Allows freedom to think, feel, want and be.
* Respects personal decisions and accepts consequences.
* Communicates directly, honestly and appropriately.
* Activates energy for producing goals.
* Communicates equality to others.
* Improves self esteem whether win, lose or draw.

MESSAGE OWNERSHIP

I MESSAGES	YOU MESSAGES
Claims Feelings	*Blames* *Behavior on Others*
Claim your feelings	Criticizes, Labels
Behavior information	Judges, Argues
Informs how you are different	Rejects

COMMUNICATIONS RESULTS

Opens	*Blocks*
Maintains Relationship	Brings Control
Helps to Solve Problems	Harms the Relationship

The most energizing part of the problem solving is a person's ability to expose pain and shame. Allowing others to see your pain is the lowest ebb in a relationship but amazingly can be the turning point. When someone decides to become authentic and expose real feelings, others come to the rescue. This is ultimately a risk factor of timing. The choice is to be true to yourself or decide to play it safe.

Self disclosure correctly informs others of your feelings immediately, appropriately, consistently, and lovingly. It values listening to yourself as important as listening to others in the communication process. "I Messages," use three elements: your feelings, the behavior that triggered your feelings, and how it affected you. These feeling messages help others to understand your pain by keeping communication open, maintaining relationships and helping solve or prevent problems. Examples: I was disappointed when you didn't call last night. I stayed home because you said you would call.

Most people take the easy route to blame others in communication. It always begins with "You!" The opposite of centering, it attempts to transfer pain to others and doesn't accept responsibility in the communication. It is judgment, rejecting, controlling, blocks communication and continues the hurt. Example: You let me down last night, you didn't call, I'll never stay home for you again.

LISTENING TO UNDERSTAND, NOT GIVING ANSWERS

The most important behavior in communication is listening: the ability to hear a person's authentic self. There are three positive benefits when you listen correctly A listener must use the self-discipline of patience which builds trust in both parties because it's an honor to hear someone's story. Good listening gives self esteem to both parties. The listener's gift of time is rewarded by the obvious change in another person's attitude and direction because the generous act of listening helps another find his path again.

Listening has several simple skills which, when added together, helps people gain competencies. The three roles of a listener are: as a student—you learn new material, as a sensitive sage—to comfort troubled people and as a guidance director—to confront uncomfortable situations. Effective listening is a process of many things, but always has a deep respectful interest in the other person, and uses gentle questions to probe the layers of a situation.

TUNING IN

To

Others Feelings

"We need to get
this situation
out in the open."

Comforting troubled people is time consuming and hard work. Many people resist the time needed to comfort others. **Once the skills are learned, comforting listening is a time saver, and is the easiest, simplest and quickest route to take.** When you hear a person's woes, and help them regain control, they are less likely to return. People need others to simply vent frustration occasionally.

The listener who comforts needs patience to draw out the other person's problem properly and then mirrors back to the speaker the feelings. When you identify you can empathize, The listener must announce the feeling to them: "**You must have felt _____.**" As simple as this is, helping the person to identify feelings is essential in the listening process. Next explore several alternatives and you may even give some ideas at this time, then inquire, "What have you decided to do?" The comforting process is complete when the two following guidelines have been accomplished: the person has something new to do and they feel better. The troubled person must solve the problem. Self confidence is decreased when others do for them what they need to do for themselves.

Confrontation skills are more flexible because sometimes you must listen to your partner, then change to listen to yourself. The key in conflict listening is: you have the problem. A man gave this synopsis of his marital success: "My wife and I agreed that only one of us could be mad at a time." More on the confrontation process later.

EMOTIONAL ANTENNAE

In a truly nurturing relationship, the emotional antennae is tuned so the partner's mood can be monitored. In his book "American Couples," Phillip Blumstein wrote, "A satisfying marriage is almost guaranteed when the three elements of nurturing, attention and time are exchanged between partners." When you feel someone is uncomfortable or hiding something, you go to the trouble to ask leading questions to find the source of pain. This "digging it out" is a sensitive, probing kind of listening which helps people unload.

Often times, people may not want to talk. They may even resist conversation for awhile. But when the timing is right, go back to the situation and gently remind them that life is not normal and you need to talk: "*I'm not happy until you are okay.*" This probing sets the stage for things to be brought out into discussion. Sometimes you simply announce, "We need to get this situation out in the open."

GOOD LISTENERS

respect the need
for others
to vent without telling
them what to do.

RESIST GIVING ANSWERS

There are those who listen with an agenda. They see listening as a process of giving information instead of understanding the other's crisis. **Good listening simply do not give answers**. Instead they respect the other's need for venting to reflect behavior so they can solve simple problems for themselves.

The interpersonal communication process requires the expression of a sender and the impressions of a receiver. Effective communication improves self-esteem immediately, maintains the relationship, and enhances the quality of life in the long run.

As the saying goes, *"it's not what you say, it's the way you say it."* No wonder people have trouble trying to communicate. Instead of dealing with issues and solving problems, the implication of many messages are "I'm the parent and you're the child," "I'm right and you are wrong," or "You're stupid and I am smart."

The listener can also respond incorrectly. Listeners get defensive, sometime they feel, "I've heard this before," and simply turn off listening. This, in essence, is an answer; the person is not worthy of their time!

RESIST RETALIATION

Refrain from saying hurtful things to your partner. Learn to bite your tongue. It's acceptable to think ugly, terrible acts of violence, it's quite another to say or carry them out. Resentful remarks escalate the fight as would pouring gas on a burning fire. Labeling and name calling are "no no's" in relationship, and only erode the fragile bank account of trust. This lengthens the war, causing partners to stray from the issues to defend themselves. Attacking those who think differently than you isn't respectful. Use self discipline to hold your tongue on vengeful remarks when the partner says something inappropriate. A listening response would be "I don't appreciate you attacking my character, can we get to the issues instead?"

In my classroom, we reminded each other not to use "put downs." Students had developed habits of name-calling when it wasn't funny! I called a halt to the long standing problem by teaching young people to recognize any negativity in anyone including the teacher. This unusual method worked! In two weeks time, we had a safe classroom; putdowns and name calling were not allowed in class.

STRATEGIES

- ❖ COLLABORATE

- ❖ COMPROMISE

- ❖ ACCOMMODATE

- ❖ COMPETITIVE

- ❖ AVOIDANCE

Chapter 7

COPING STRAGEGIES

THE COPING STRATEGIES

There are five coping strategies, all of which involve varying degrees of self esteem, coping skills of self disclosure, listening and commitment to the partner. The strategies are collaboration, compromise, accommodation, competition and avoidance. The conflict patterns reflected in the these strategies are to: (1) **agree**, (2) **agree to disagree**, (3) **disagree**.

Relationships work well when both people agree. Years ago, a friend anticipated disagreement about returning to college to finish a master's degree program. It was the first time of many that that her husband said to her, "If it makes you happy, it makes me happy."

FIRST STRATEGY: COLLABORATION

We need to know that the most important coping strategy is collaboration. Collaboration creates a reciprocity that you cannot purchase anywhere. This strategy depends on mutual problem solving, trust, openness and supportive communication climate. It satisfies people's deepest needs. People who are collaborators have high self esteem, high regard for others and good coping skills.

Collaboration uses synergy, a refined energy where two heads work better than one. Defined as the sum being greater than its parts, synergy works with people's strengths. Music played together is more beautiful than when played alone. Spirited, creative, loving relationships produce wonderful results.

Stephen Covey in his book, <u>Seven Habits of Highly Effective People</u>, recommends three behaviors to affect this positive change. Integrity is the ability to keep your work while maturity involves the courage to bring forth uncomfortable issues, and prosperity recognizes there is enough to go around. When people grasp the attitude of fun in their projects, an emotional bank account of trust develops. It is fun knowing how to make work seem like play.

5 STYLES OF COPING

COLLABORATORS
High Self Interest
High Others Interest
Good Coping Skills

COMPETITION
High Self
Low Others
Good ProblemSkills

COMPROMISE
Mutual Self Interest
Mutual Others
Medium Problem

ACCOMPLISHING
High Self
Low Others
Low Problem Concern

AVOIDANCE
Low Self Interest
Low Others Interest
Low ProblemInterest

SECOND STRATEGY COMPROMISING

Compromising deals with fairness, sharing and taking turns. It partially satisfies each other's needs rather than neither having a piece of the pie. It's finding the middle ground from which to operate, it's one umbrella keeping two people apart half dry. Some situations do not lend to a win-win, there may be some loss for both parties. This compromise protects continuing a relationship.

We need to compromise time and money. We can go to different movies or compromise; you choose now, and the next time is my choice. In negotiations, we may get certain items or we can split a percentage of 60/40 or 50/50. We can't have it all, we have to divide. Compromise can include situations where we agree to disagree: I get Crest and you get Colgate. Compromise has a mutual concern for self, others and the problems involved.

THIRD STRATEGY: COMPETING

Competing is known as I win—you lost script. Winning at the expense of others is taught from a early age. Instead of a cooperative spirit, someone wins and others have to lose. Based on the attitude of scarcity, it teaches there is not enough to go around. Competing invites you to feel good when you win, consequently you feel badly when you lose. Competition encourages selfishness, not giving and receiving. Tests and childhood games train for the competitive skills. Many families embrace competitiveness because that is the way the business world and school operate.

There are two kinds of competitions, personal and group. We need a certain amount of personal competitive spirit to deal with the struggle in life. Having a positive internal competitive spirit helps us set goals and recognize our progress toward them. Competitive people have high self regard, low concern for others and negative interest in the problem.

FOURTH STRATEGY: ACCOMMODATING

Accommodating is known as "I lose—you win." Others needs become more important than our own, which have low priority. This sacrificial person will do for others then do without themselves. The roles of parenting, nursing and ministry emphasize this selfless behavior, all of which have the core of making a difference in many lives. The distinction is, in excess, the other person winds up with low self esteem.

AVOIDANCE BEHAVIORS

MANIPULATION

BLAMING

HONESTY FREEDOM

AWARENESS TRUST

DEPENDANCY

PROTECTION

DEPENDANCY

PROTECTION

Many people accommodate others because they have not adequately defined their own goals. Secondly, they need to learn to say "No," as well as respect more from others for themselves personally. "You get yours" emphasizes agreement but avoids confrontation. People who continually accommodate others have a high concern for others, low concern for self and low problem solving skills.

FIFTH STRATEGY: AVOIDANCE

Individuals who avoid others operate from a position of withdrawal, apathy, abdication and failure. This is the most aggravating stance because people refuse to fight. Avoidance could be called missing the mark while delivering a message. These people tend to speak indirectly instead of straight to the issue. They work from a negative point of reference. When I was in the second grade at a spring pageant, my partner and I were the lead couple in a song "Coming Through the Rye." This old Scottish refrain stayed with me all these years of "*you take the high road and I'll take the low road*" to mean that some take a positive attitude while others pursue a negative attitude in life.

The four sub strategies of protection, manipulation, blaming and dependency are the negative roads of a life while the expositive roads become honesty instead of manipulation, freedom instead of blaming, trust instead of protection, and awareness instead of dependency. The visuals shown describe avoidance strategies and the key messages they transmit. The avoidance strategies operate using low self esteem, low concern for others and low coping ability.

We **protect** people because we don't trust them to handle life as well as we can. Protective people would rather do it themselves than confront others. The results can be disastrous: over-protective people become unreliable because their ability to trust themselves or be trusted has been reduced. They have not been trusted to handle responsibility. The key boundary involves recognizing we must not allow others to protect us. Symbolized by a Steve Martin type narrow hat, an amusing art form saying "Go talk to someone else, not me." The key message to the protector says "trust others to deal with their problems."

Manipulators are deceptive, selfish and controlling. Manipulators core problem is they are cunningly selfish, and they always want something for nothing. We all get involved with people who want to control us at times. Because the

AVOIDANCE COPING STRATEGIES

PROTECTION

MANIPULATION

BLAMING

DEPENDENCY

manipulator may use pleasantries, the victim assumes the relationship is equal and becomes hooked into pleasing the other. Without realizing it, victims become dependent and controlled. A key boundary in dealing with a manipulator is deciding "I will not be a victim." Recognize your own worth and bring everything out in the open. The message to them is, "Don't take an unfair advantage."

Blamers try to avoid taking responsibility for their action by blaming others. This behavior will continue as long as they can get away with it! This irresponsibility is the dance we call sidetracking. Blamers intimidate their partners, causing them to want to escape. In relationships, the attacked victim becomes overwhelmed by the aggressiveness and often is quiet, frustrated, and may even leave. Blaming causes the partner to be afraid to express oneself. The key boundary in dealing with a blamer is not accepting ownership of the problem. The key message for the blamer is, "Relax, mistakes are okay."

Dependency is refusing to grow up, but instead letting others act for them. Dependency is the inability to be a whole separate person and one of the underlying causes of chemical abuse, hero worship or the "clinging vine" in relationships. The dependent's need is overwhelming and creates a desperate attempt to hang on to others. The key boundary in dealing with dependents is "tough love." The core problem is the inability to love themselves. The key message to the person who plays Peter Pan is: "Have the courage to be a whole person."

THE
FIGHT RECIPE

Look at each comment
      as having unfriendly ulterior motives!
Defend yourself by criticizing them.

Recall all past criticism, saying,
      "You always or you never!
Recite sacrifices made for the other.

Work for control of the conversation.

Taunt the other person into anger.

Embarrass them with their behavior.

Resume the squabble quickly.

Chapter 8

COPING METHODS THAT WORK

THE FIGHT RECIPE

The amusing fight recipe helps us looks at the particular behaviors involved in keeping the fight alive. Life is more than keeping score on relationships battles. By examining methods used we will be able to change them. "You have asked me the way and I have shown you. But I, too am a traveler myself and in helping you I have gone far beyond myself." as George Bernard Shaw stated. This book sorts through practical methods to help you know how to keep an emotional perspective during conflict.

SELF ESTEEM AND CONFLICT

Self image defines our love-hate relationship with ourselves. Self esteem means we like who we are. The more we love ourselves, the easier to bridge our differences with others. The more difficulty with appreciating differences, the poorer our self image. To keep our self esteem high we learn to handle conflict so both parties feel good.

COPING MEANS WORKING AS EQUALS

Coping methods help balance the power difficult people have over you. Coping methods are a combination of the self disclosure and listening skills but also the intuitive knowledge of when to use the methods and techniques described below. It includes leveling, timing, appointments, the place of conflict, focus ownership, using humor, and even setting future boundaries. Learning to cope also means upgrading your coping strategy.

According to Robert Bramson's book, Coping with Difficult People, there are difficult people who are hostile, bossy people who steam and spew, gripers and grunters who pour cold water on your ideas and plans. Some peoples project icy or lukewarm behaviors that leave you confused and you never know where you stand. **We need to relate with these difficult people differently.**

COPING METHODS

- **LEVELING**

- **TIMING**

- **APPOINTMENTS**

- **CONFLICT PLACE**

- **FOCUS**

- **OWNERSHIP**

- **DETOURING**

- **BOUNDARIES**

- **HUMOR**

Coping means "working as equals." Many relationships are not equal. *"Coping methods interfere with previous 'successful' functioning of the behavior. Passive behavior produces a double cost to the individual: a feeling of martyrdom (Look at how much I am doing) and the continued hated behavior in the other person,"* states Bramson.

LEVELING

To deal with behavior different than our own, we must adjust our behavior to match their methods. This leveling eventually will help reduce the tension. If a person is soft spoken, lower your volume to make your point to them. When a baby hits you, they will understand when you grab and hold their hand. People who are aggressive will walk over people who are meek, they will respect those who are equally demanding and curt.

Leveling involves adapting our behavior to get their attention. As long as we are inflexible, our ability to get along with others is reduced. We go to other people's level to teach, to sell, and to influence. That includes almost every profession and family situation, doesn't it? As the newspaper columnist Jim Bishop wrote, "There is no way out but through." Leveling works to reach equilibrium.

CONFLICT RESOLUTION IS SIMPLE BUT NOT EASY

Conflict resolution is simple but the issues of conflict focus and the commitment to continue the relationship. Inform the partner what you want and don't want. Since we can only change ourselves, deal with what you can do and let go of the issues you can't change. It may help to sleep on the possibilities to get a more balanced solution to evolve.

After you both agree there is problem and a commitment to resolve it, then and only then can you apply the problem of solving "who—does what—when" formula. Many projects fail because of lack of follow through. An evaluation to check the progress or what needs discussion later must be part of resolving problems.

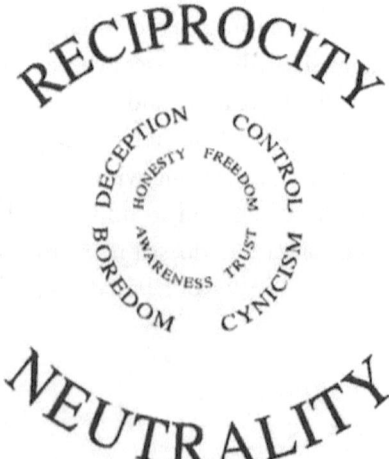

CONFLICT NEEDS

RECIPROCITY

DECEPTION CONTROL
HONESTY FREEDOM
AWARENESS TRUST
BOREDOM CYNICISM

NEUTRALITY

CONTRASTED

You can't rush decisions. Crisis decisions cut down the options available to the person. As outsiders, we often look at another person's plight and see many possibilities. There are two real choices: to stay or leave? Staying may mean to suffer but also to hope, to argue or open up, to resolve issues and move on with your life. One can leave the conversation, or go for a walk around the block. Some leave emotionally but stay physically, others decide to leave permanently, some people stay to make others suffer.

CONSTRUCTIVE CONFLICT

People don't know their inner strengths until tested. It's when the going gets tough that a person' character develops and emerges. When Maslow stated that the self actualizor developed the four positive qualities of honesty, awareness, freedom and trust within himself, he gave the signposts for constructive conflict as well.

Construction conflict requires both reciprocity and neutrality. **Reciprocity** means both parties participate in the matter and makes sure messages are understood. This not only includes listening to the other person and the ability to disclose sensitive feelings about self, but also the ability to receive feedback about your behavior. Practicing reciprocity assures fairness which includes **awareness and trust**. Sharing experiences honestly causes us to trust that the other person is also working to improve the "us." Both can stretch to toward new growth, unless someone maintains stubbornness and resists.

Neutrality can best described as a "cool head." To retain a neutral emotional balance includes not judging when, where or what is said. **Being honest and allowing freedom** comes from becoming nonjudgmental; a valuable, learnable skill. Neutrality gives people time to think instead of jumping to conclusions, and helps objectivity. Becoming objective helps you respect their opinions as relevant as you own. You realize the other person is your teacher. There is something you don't understand about them and your patience will help clear it up. By continuing patience, you will smother aggression into a smoldering ember until you see the entire situation differently and can then work together to arrive at a solution. Another important aspect of neutrality is the development of tolerance, a stance of calmness over small issues to work on larger ones. It is the larger picture we are working to see. Of course, some people make a mountain out of a molehill, they focus on the trivial instead the bigger picture of working together.

"Can we talk?"

TIMING

Just as comedians, politicians and lovers all know the importance of timing, so should those who have a legitimate conflict to negotiate. There is a great need for perspective when you are angry. We can interrupt our angry cycle. Angry people need to cool down before taking a grievance to a person. Therefore we say: count to 10, or go for a walk to cool down, since distance helps us gain perspective.

Not only do we need to recognize the anger in ourselves, but also realize when is the best time to approach others. Teenagers are swift in recognizing to ask for the car or money when we feel good. Their timing is perfect. We need to be aware when parents are tired, sick or overwhelmed with other matters. Sometimes it might be better for us to postpone a discussion until a more appropriate time.

Because postponing discussions can aggravate a bad situation, making an appointment to talk is a prime investment in the relationship. We often hold on to a problem until we are truly normal at all. We must interrupt our schedule long enough to discuss problems. Like Joan Rivers, we need to ask, "Can we talk?"

THE APPOINTMENT

Saying "Can we talk?" is easy for some, for others discussion of deep issues with significant people require an attention getter. Years ago a boy came into my office and stated, "I am on the verge of becoming a criminal." He had committed burglary with some fellows who were about to commit more. "I've been involved in some smaller things but it's going to get bigger. It scares me but not as much as what is going on at home!" Mark continued, "When I was 14 years old, I ran away from home. I was gone for five months for the first time. When I came back I thought things were going to be better.

Now, three years later, when I walk in the door, my Mama tells me everything I've done wrong: the police, the school, my choice of friends, my report card, what I do and don't do at home. On and on she goes, until I just can't take it anymore. I know my Mama loves me but I think my buddies care more about me than she does. I can't stand her constant criticism!" With eyes blazing, Mark continued, "I'd like to hit her, but you can't hit your Mama. I can take so much and then I'm gone. The only thing I know to do is leave. I'm out the door by 4:00 pm., and I don't come home before Mama is in bed."

THE APPOINTMENT

"When it's convenient for you, I have a problem I would like to discuss"

The boy had a problem. He was worried about how to get his point across to his Mama so we composed and he practiced the following message: "**Mother, when it's convenient for you, I have a problem I would like to discuss**." It worked like a charm for Mark to confront his mother just before he went to school. This FOCUS technique is helpful to develop the courage of pent up feelings; this is very helpful in planting the seeds of real discussion so you can balance the under-dog role and redeem your self esteem. Mark made peace with his mother and eventually found new friends.

PLACE

Find the appropriate place to have a conflict. When a personal relationship interrupts work, the employer-employee role is threatened. Jeannine's boyfriend called her work and demanded to know to whom she was talking prior to his phone call. The person was still standing there on a business matter and it became increasingly uncomfortable to talk to the boyfriend and perform her office role. The social scene is just as disheartening; friends interfere or make assumptions that aren't necessarily true.

Request privacy away from other for discussions—a car, home, or the kitchen. A neutral spot where *neither party* has territorial ownership may offer addition benefits for a fairer fight; a park, or a restaurant may work better than a family place.

STAYING FOCUSED ON THE PROBLEM

Focus is essential in conflict resolution. Staying focused means not bringing up other unresolved issues at the moment. This conflict is the only situation to resolve now. Staying focused keeps your energy on this problem. Many people use a shotgun approach, "If this isn't going my way, I'll show you how wrong you are by dragging up past a battle to shoot you down." When a partner drags up other issues it's an attempt to dilute the message they do not want to accept. To illustrate: As was his summer pattern, a husband golfed on weekends and his days off. His wife worked evening hours with Sundays being their only family day. She used Sundays to browse in the local department store while he golfed, and on one occasion she went alone to watch a enactment of an old battle in a public park.

Upon her return her husband was livid about her going to a park without him. He was angry because he felt it was unsafe. He also had objected to the department store browsing and implied she might be looking for men! The woman's

FOCUS

- **Problem ownership**

- **Sidetracking efforts**

- **Detour statements**

- **New boundaries**

frustration increased due to the lack of trust and freedom of choice when he wasn't available. (This could be many families fight!) It's difficult to stay fair and neutral as a male thing! What does the female have to solve the problem? First, she could beg to understand her side of the issue. Second, she could attack his absence. Third, she could neutralize her anger by allowing him to own the problem.

Who owns the problem? It depends on which one has not convinced the other of his or her needs.

REDIRECT SIDETRACKING

Aggressiveness is intimidating. A pointed finger, or shouted vulgarities are scare tactics that increase polarization. Such methods move discussions from the issue to the personality. The conflict should be about the issue, not personalities. Using threats to intimidate doesn't solve problems, it only compounds them. Problems can be solved.

Nothing is more upsetting than to confront someone on an issue and they fire back! What to do? Most of us begin the defensive route of "I'm sorry" and wish we had never begun this degrading conversation. We feel lost after opening an issue of importance only to get turned around and become the victim. Because no one wants to have their weaknesses and poor judgments brought to light, when you bring up a situation, the other person's natural behavior is to defend themselves by attacking something about you. When someone attacks you while presenting a problem, keep to the original issue.

This "**sidetracking**," switching blame from one to another, creates confusion. The attacked person can learn to say to the other person nicely, "That's not the issue at this time, this is the problem." The ability to call a person's bluff about your personality is a skill well worth mastering. When attacked, staying in neutral gear is a healthy way to keep focused on the problem solving. Even when they speak to distract the pressure on them, work the conversation back to the issues. Postpone those unrelated discussions with refocusing statements like: "Let's discuss that later," or "We'll deal with that after we settle this issue."

Staying focused has additional merits. When this problem is resolved, life can resume as normal. We recognize a basic truth; for every minute you're mad, you lose sixty seconds of happiness. Who wants to live like that?

GIVING AWAY THE PROBLEM

- **CREATE**
  an appetizer to talk

- **MAKE**
  an appointment

- **SHRUGG**
  off blaming remarks

- **RESPOND**
  by focusing on problem

- **STAY**
  level emotionally

When a quarrel reaches an impasse between two people, one critical stage is "Who owns the problem?" Back off objectively to ask the following question. **Who has not convinced the other of their needs**? When you are frustrated with an issue, it's even more upsetting to know they don't listen. Find a way to finish the problem solving. Don't be **sidetracked**. They ignore your confrontation yet want you to accept theirs! How do you handle that? Refuse to accept their accusations by ignoring or postponing them.

Another method we use is detouring. **Detouring** allows another issue to be brought into the conversation without defending it, Instead, respond with, "You may be right about that, let us speak to that issue at another time," or "Let's deal with that issue later." You have correctly recovered from the detour when the conversation comes back to the main issue. Instead of accepting the sidetracking problem, give them a problem. Use the non-blaming method of "I messages," to share information so they can consider changing their behavior. Do you want to be rid of your frustration? Accept and claim your problem. That doesn't mean to ignore theirs but keep to your issue without being dismissed.

HUMOR

Humor is the purest intellectual form of problem solving. The person skilled in a witty response can turn a phrase, and spin a negative attitude into a positive or more healthy one. It's difficult to stay angry with people who take the light approach, who turn things around so people smile instead of taking the attack position. One student shared his parents' process for peace making: The mother becoming icily silent, walking around without speaking or smiling, the father following her from room to room, repeating, "Toots, please! You're not going to be mad at me, are you?" Finally, the wife, who couldn't stay mad with this puppy dog approach, would grin. The husband responded "Toots, I sure am glad you forgive me."

People who use humor have learned not to get excited over every issue. Most things can be put on the back burner just to keep things from exploding, In the book The Art of War, the Japanese war lords recognized centuries ago that it is permissible to lose battles to order to win a war.

BOUNDARIES

Sets New Limitations

- Separate the person
    from the problem.

- Identify problem ownership.

- Admit annoying behavior quickly.

- Change your reaction
    to alter their behavior.

- Recognize when others resist change.

- Neutralize feelings so others
    can't push your buttons.

- Always take loving care of yourself.

WHO OWNS THE PROBLEM

* Separate the person from the problem.
* Identify who owns problem.
* Admit annoying behavior quickly.
* Change your reaction to alter their behavior.
* Recognize when others resist change.
* Neutralize feelings so others can no longer push your buttons.
* Always take loving care of yourself.

Setting boundaries are the mental gymnastics when we personally need to make changes. It helps separate the person from the problem. Delaying the process so others can no longer push your buttons is healthy. Realizing what you can't tolerate in relationships becomes as important as what you want. If you don't know what you want, you can be manipulated into someone else's agenda. Setting boundaries will help you make a stand. These inner controls are based on an individual's own sense of right and wrong, values, priorities and personal life experiences.

We find it difficult to own the problem. As a little girl my daddy would tickle me until I said "Stop." Other relatives tickled me and continued where it was painful and I would cry. Not everyone listened to "Stop." That is the predicament when people are not sensitive to our pain; they continue as usual. I removed myself from the situation so I could not be tickled when those relatives came around. As a child I did not discuss the situation, I got away.

The general rule is we cannot make anyone do anything! But the amended rule is "Yes, you can, when you stop responding to their needs." People will continue until you remove your help. When you stop, people sometimes understand you are not the same, and this helps them recognize when and how they have offended you. You must do two things: first you must act differently and then secondly, discuss what you need from them. People are not mind readers; they need help in understanding what change you need, just as you need help from them. Discussion works better than silence and has a better way of ending resentments.

Setting boundaries is a self esteem issue. When we decide we are worthwhile and have value, we also decide to be treated in a respectful manner. Setting boundaries is recognizing our area of authority and defining internally how we will be treated. It has nothing to do with confronting others.

COPING

Involves Using

The skills Of

SELF DISCLOSURE

GOOD LISTENING

METHODS

TECHNIQUES

STRATEGY

SETTING NEW BOUNDARIES

Kaye described how her job changed when a new boss took over. The behaviors previously in place were suddenly taboo, alliances once solid began to crumble, and behaviors once freely exchanged were not allowed. The working structure that once was relaxed, productive and fun became rigid, hostile and separate. She didn't like it and considered quitting.

Kaye had difficulty adjusting to change. It created an inner conflict. Like Kaye, we enjoy things the way they are. Even though not perfect, conditions were comfortable and familiar. We don't have all the answers and we have to keep working on adjusting.

Gradually, Kaye came to realize that she was feeling hooked by the new boss's behavior and felt threatened and controlled. To prevent losing her ability to function and do her work, it became necessary to change her attitude toward the work situation and the boss. Kaye reported a growth spurt in herself as a result of the tumultuous change.

Some adjustments came from focusing on good parts of the change rather than the negative aspects. Keeping to the clock had given her more free time, not less. Kaye's new boundary was letting go of resentment. She didn't like herself for holding on to the grudges. She asked herself: What does it matter? It doesn't!, she decided. She started singing the old song You've Got to Accentuate the Positive! It worked.

PROBLEM SOLVING SKILLS

Learning to confront involves two key skills 1) The skill of self disclosure identifies and expresses feelings, and works to be understood. Self disclosure values feelings enough to tell the truth. 2) Secondly it is being able to listen to others, to understand and comfort their pain but also the ability to confront your problems by listening to yourself. In the next chapter, we deal with confrontation, the ability to feel your own pain and the willingness to act upon it.

CONFRONTATION PROCESS

Recognize need for change.

Gain thoughtful perspective.

Set personal boundaries.

Practice confronting others.

Make an appointment.

Confront the person.
(who—what—when—where)

Allow adjustment time.

Chapter 9

LEARNING TO GIVE YOUR
PROBLEM TO OTHERS

FACING PROBLEMS

One embarrassing episode on the first visit home after marriage taught me how manipulation can backfire. Both mothers asked the same question: "Well, how are you two getting along?" With my mother, I was smart enough to state positive things about my new husband. To my mother-in-law, I described her son's negative attitude about housework. I knew her feminine instincts would encourage her to urge her son to be more helpful with tasks.

Sure enough not long after, she and her son went into a bedroom to chat. My husband was polite, but on the return trip he pounced upon the subject of being disgraced in his parents eyes. Eventually I got the point. I had manipulated the scene so someone else could fight my battles for me.

Manipulation is an unhealthy decision because it undermines both people's problem solving abilities. This buried anger blames, controls, and destroys self esteem. Sandie, a former student, continued to run away instead of facing problems. After she married, she attempted to run away when she and her husband disagreed about disciplining a child. She caught herself in the midst of panic and recognized her need to face people and share her frustrated anger in calm conversation.

We often don't want to face our problems; we would rather run away or have others fight for us. Unfortunately it simply doesn't work. We need to have the courage to deal directly with those with whom we have the most difficulty; our mates, children, parents, friends or co-workers.

THE COURAGE TO CONFRONT

The most difficult coping skill in relationships is the courage to confront. It is listening to your own pain and becoming honest enough to share it. Confrontation means coming face to face with a person or situation. But once we learn how, it becomes much easier.

WHY CONFRONTATION
IS NECESSARY

I don't want your problems!

You have to ask!

You may have to persist.

It means you communicate the problem to the other person. People don't want our problems! I don't want your problems: I have enough problems without your interrupting my life and wanting my involvement. (However, I might be convinced!) You have to ask! Think of a problem as similar to a ping pong game: the ball gets bounced back and forth between partners. But someone misses the play, drops the ball. Similarly in a relationship, the ball gets tossed into a corner and is dropped. You must interest the partner in playing with you again.

CONFRONTATION

Friendly confrontation is the specific skill needed to face a person. You must recognize the need for a change because you value the relationship. Solitude may help you gain composure and focus your thoughts. As much as you dread it, you also recognize the important of an opportunity to open a discussion. It is good to practice what you want to say. Long standing issues need clarity. Sometimes a trusted neutral person may help you see a new way to present an issue.

When it's a situation of long standing buried resentment, it may be good to make the appointment, then leave before having the conversation. Setting an appointment will get you going. Rather than a surprise tactic, present the confrontation first as a future discussion: "I have something to discuss," or "We need to talk soon."

Share positive information before the main topic of interest. People have a tendency to believe negative information if you start with three or more honest statements of fact. During the confrontation, the conversation must focus on the issue, on observations or on specific incidents that created the uncomfortable feelings.

At the time of the confrontation say: "I am uncomfortable with (name the specific behavior)." Then **SHUT UP**! Allow the person to feel your pain. Most of us butt in before the person has digested the confrontation. Since people will deny, belittle or minimize the issue, you may need to ask "If you continue this behavior will it make our relationship better or worse?" Then say : "(Name) Do you want our relationship to get better or worse?" When they try to divert the pressure, stay focused. Allow time and space for them to recognize the problem. Forgive them even if they don't accept it the first time. Create an atmosphere of importance, privacy, appropriateness to accept the situation and, in time, others will respond to your needs.

DEAL

Discuss your need to talk—
     state things clearly.

Empathize—see things
     from their vantage point.

Announce feelings—
     self disclose your pain.

Listen deeply—
     "Tell me more," or
     "You're feeling _____?"

FIRST CONFRONTATIONS ARE THE HARDEST

The first time I remember honestly sharing my frustration with someone else's behavior (outside my family) was with my roommate in college. The great problem was the laundry! As new roommates, our fall schedules had similar free time so we made a mutual decision to do laundry on Wednesdays. The following semester our schedules changed but I continued to do the laundry as usual.

Before realizing how it came to be, I was seething with resentment for her not finding time for the laundry occasionally. I was truly upset! When I confronted her, she let me have a mouthful about how I misjudged the situation. "You've got your nerve," she said, "I never ask you to do my laundry!" In my first confrontation, I was annoyed with her for not recognizing my contribution.

Looking back, I did my more than my share and was actually playing the martyr's role. I simply did my own washing during those semesters when our schedules clashed. We found clearing the air difficult, but our friendship became stronger because we had solved our differences which renewed our faith in each other.

Use the DEAL formula to become better at confronting others.

* Discuss your need to talk—state things clearly.
* Empathize—see things from the other's vantage point.
* Announce feelings—self disclose your pain.
* Listen deeply—"Tell me more," or "Your feeling _____."

FINER POINTS OF CONFRONTATION

The secret skill of confrontation is refusing to quit. The persistence of finding another way to resolve the problem takes real skill. However, in relationships you must go back and renegotiate the problem with the other person. This may not be the best time or place or method to produce the results you need. Discussing what didn't work and other avenues of reconciliation with a trusted friend is a very good tactic.

What else can you do? Sometimes a written outline is helpful to prioritize the details of a grievance. In very stressful situations, a written letter can be very helpful. Giving the whole story of thought conveyed without being interrupted, and you can give your whole train of thought, then edit it until it is clear. When the other person receives the written request for change, with enough time for reflection they may come back to resolve the issue.

Sometimes

"LETTING GO"

Is the best coping
decision to make!

There is growing scientific evidence that venting your anger through crying, which women are more inclined to do, provides a safety net in emotional maintenance. Deep feelings may make us sad. Everyone may not agree on this, but many people allow themselves to have a good cry before proceeding after a deep disappointment or frustration. With their tensions somewhat relieved, they feel better, they have a better perspective and can then be more rational in the situation.

INTERVENTION

Intervention is a step beyond confrontation. It interrupts a serious behavioral problem that is out of hand. It's purpose is an invitation to grow, to develop potential and a nudge to move toward maturity. It's only done with love and uses "tough love tactics." It's the courage to let the person see how they are coming across when they are blind to the consequences. Intervention is usually done with more than one person. A family intervention proceeds to help a person see the results of drinking, drugs or unhealthy relationships.

The friendly intervention help others feel cherished and stimulated to learn. It encourages them to examine their mistakes and prevents drifting, stagnation, or wandering from their inner potential. Peer pressure works, but it must be agreed what to do, when, where and how to approach the situation.

Betty Ford's family confronted her with the pain of her drinking behavior. It takes time to break through the person's denial. That's why it must it must be orchestrated to be long enough for the person to run through each excuse and be confronted on each one, then have no way out except to admit there is a problem.

LETTING GO

Once in a great while, things have gone on too long and there may not be a reconciliation. Sometimes, people don't respond to the confrontation and want out of a relationship. Although most decisions are best decided mutually, it's important to respect another person's decision even though you feel it's not in your best interests. There is the law of reversed effort that also can be applied here. Having done all, STOP. Quit trying. Sometimes we work too hard and when we quit, suddenly the forces of nature start moving again. I don't know why, it just is. I can't explain gravity either.

CONFRONTING TOPICS

WHAT is the issue?

WHO has the problem?

WHERE do you fight?

WHEN do you battle?

NEVER ASK WHY?

Why questions create confusion, frustration, and duplicity.

WHAT MAKES A GOOD FIGHT

In my first marriage, there were few skirmishes. I remember the normal adjustments, but no real toe-to-toe arguments in our twenty five years of marriage before he died—except one life changing fight during the week following our son's graduation. It was the best fight we ever had! Our relationship was immensely relieved when the irritating factor, a continuing problem with a friend's influence over me, was solved. My husband finally made me understand his pain by throwing down the challenge: "*You listen to everybody but me.*" The fight was loud, emotionally draining, repetitive, and accusatory. Afterwards, we had a new commitment in our marriage.

In looking at close relationships, the real purpose of fighting is growth. If either of you is unhappy, then a discussion of differences and what is causing the problems is in order. When the purpose of a fight is change, then the discussion becomes what, how, when and where. Never ask why. <u>People do not always know why they do things</u>. Although why questions are great in the scientific world, they are misleading in the realm of human relationships. **"Why"** questions lead to frustration, deception and confusion of dealing with yesterday. Stay in the present moment for this particular misunderstanding,. You may intuitively understand why and know more about the person than they realize. The point is you don't need to make them admit it to clear the air. The important material is:

* What is the issue?
* Who has the problem?
* Where do you fight?
* When do you battle?

LOVE

IS OUR

ONLY

REALITY!

Chapter 10

LOVE—THE NEED TO CONNECT

LOVE UNITES

There are only two emotions: Love unites, connects, surrenders and admits weaknesses. Love gives us that warm feeling where we are at one with the universe. It's that bubbling over of joy where you can't get a grin off your face. You want to call someone and share the news. Working on ourselves to be a more loving person will release our joy, just like water flows when we turn on the faucet.

Love is a multiplier, the more you share, the more joy you feel. Being open, honest and vulnerable is the ultimate passion. What a shock! Most people think if you share your good feelings, you are putting your head on the block for someone to chop off. And of course, they are right. Still, it's this very human emotion of vulnerability that connects us to others—their feelings of caring to love. Love is our reality. It will stay with us longer than any possession.

People have difficulty objectively. Corinthians 13, defined them well, but Paul, as a tax collector, had trouble displaying them until he had a blinding experience and saw with "new eye." The following nine character traits qualify as the foundation of the "Golden Rule" Love you neighbor as yourself."

PATIENCE—Love suffers a long time and doesn't keep records.
KINDNESS—Aware of inner needs and says "How can I help?"
GENEROSITY—Allows freedom, isn't jealous, possessive or demanding.
GOOD LISTENER—Pays deep attention, understands, is teacher.
COURTESY—Has good manners and makes things easy for you.
UNSELFISHNESS—Is encouraging to others, doesn't seek self pity.
GOOD TEMPER—Has tolerance and forgiveness when things go awry.
POSITIVE THINKING—Looks for the good, keeps a balanced perspective.
HONESTY—Isn't happy with phonies, prospers with truth and sincerity.

THE FEAR OF LOVING OTHERS

BETRAYAL

RIDICULE

REJECTION

IDENTITY

BREVITY

RECOGNIZING FEARFUL FEELINGS

Anger or rage is simply a demonstration of a fear. From my youth I decided to be passive. This coping decision served me well until I began my teaching career and young people walked all over my calm, easy going nature. One boy, the stimulus of my behavior change, climbed into a kitchen cabinet to hide, later jumped out the window and ran home!

It is difficult to have perspective when we are so angry with someone! Years ago, Dr. Martin Luther King once announced to his audience, "I don't like it when someone spits in my face and makes life difficult for me," he exclaimed, "but I can still love my fellow man." At the time I was having some difficulty with a family member and this message helped separate my hateful and loving feelings into a new balance for me. Finally I understood that I didn't have to like behaviors to relate with others.

Why don't we love more often? Intellectually we know love is more powerful than hate. We don't love others because we are afraid. We need to ask what causes us to withdraw our love, to hold back, to not admit we are born, nurtured in love and that our purpose on earth is to love others. There are five recognizable fears about loving others:

* Betrayal—they will make demands or selfishly use you.
* Ridicule—you are making a fool of yourself—people will laugh.
* Rejection—they could leave you for someone else.
* Identity—you will lose your individuality and freedom.
* Brevity—people change and in time, they will go away.

DECIDING YOUR EMOTIONS

By concentrating on your stomach you know which emotion, love or fear, you are presently experiencing. When you are feeling or expressing the emotion of love; you are calm or happy, content, laughing, and giving. When you are feeling and experiencing the emotion of fear; you are uptight, discontented or intensely loud. Both are a choice. When we decide to be loving; then positive feelings, thinking, and behaviors follow. Decisions based on a negative references produce negative results.

A family member of mine always choose to write me letter when they were mad at the world. We must assume a positive attitude to make healthy decisions even when we write a letter.

FEAR IS

FALSE

EVIDENCE

APPEARING

REAL

At first I'd want to respond with an equally self pitying letter, but I remember waiting until I felt wonderfully calm to write a response. Of course, I was younger and had no idea I had chosen the right habit pattern at the time. Being positive works, a hot head makes things difficult.

We have difficulty recognizing our value as a human being. Self love accepts those tasks we do well and politely refuses those that make us feel uncomfortable. It's remarkable to discover that when you entrust yourself with self love, you realize that the self and love are the same. Making that connection can transform your life!

CENTERING: FINDING THE LOVE WITHIN YOURSELF

Problems in life are manifestations of fear. When fear appears it's simply "False Evidence Appearing Real." Rediscover the love in your life by using the "Centering" process to overcome the fear. People operate beautifully when they are in tune with their own loving thoughts and behavior, and realize they want self esteem!

The first defined act of "Centering" is to decide to look for and find the good in someone. The second act is appreciating and being glad for your fear! If you have discomfort, be grateful; it proves you are alive (dead people don't have problems). It offers an opportunity to get out of a rut; to grow and become a larger and more serene person.

Thirdly, question your loving behavior. Have you been **honest**? Did you **allow freedom** to the other party? As you became **aware** of the situation, did you think how to rebuild the **trust**?

Centering helps you focus, and captures immediate peace. To recognize it's merit, simply practice it. Take a few moments to define or write the negative feeling troubling you. Close your eyes and recognize thoughts about it as you go through the experience. Continue saying aloud until you feel it: "I take total responsibility for my contribution to the situation." Say to yourself: "Neither he/she nor I am right or wrong, we simply see this differently," or "I need to get some perspective to realign my thinking."

I used the words from Mary Martin's song to teach loving attitudes: "*A bell is no bell til you ring it, a song is no song til you sing it, and love in your heart wasn't meant there to stay, love isn't love' til you give it away.*"

Greeks Definition of

LOVE

EROS

PHILE

AGAPE

We changed the classroom environment by making it a game, we corrected negative remarks and only accepted positive remarks to create a love prosperity.

Love prosperity is: saying kind, helpful words, asking for help, giving compliments and sharing feelings about self.

Love poverty is: saying cruel words, never asking for help, rejecting compliments, sharing thinking instead of feelings.

LOVE IS THE ANSWER

Love is the major problem solver of all time. Which it is! However, do we always mean the same messages when we speak of love? The Greeks used three words to define various emotional love ties.

* **Eros**—is the personal experience of the senses, hence we say: We enjoy music, the smell of bread, watching a sunset, erotic feelings of sexuality come from this dimension of love.
* **Phile**—comes from the concept of brotherly love, includes accepting strengths and weaknesses, it's unconditional love.
* **Agape**—is the spiritual connection, the bonding of people even beyond the physical experience.

PRAISE AND ENCOURAGEMENT

Praise can be healthy or manipulative depending on whether it is used as a gift or as barter. Praising the performance rather the person can be a great encouragement. When I was 15 years old, I received a wonderful compliment from an Arkansas 4-H leader working with me. He said: "*Shirley, I love your enthusiasm.*" As state song leader, he inspired me by telling me to bend my knees to give me energy to the audience, if I stiffened my knees, it would scare me. I performed with ease before 10,000 people.

As I bent my knees I could feel the energy coming through my body to the audience, they responded and thus the audience and I had a *giving and receiving cycle* going. This message eventually transformed me into a confident public speaker. My enthusiasm, which in Greek means "life within," catches fire and always returns to me.

FORGIVENESS

is the essence of working back to equality!

Chapter 11

FORGIVENESS—THE NEED TO RESTORE EQUALITY

FORGIVENESS—A DECISION TO STAY AN EQUAL

Robert was a much loved child, but his father died when he was in the fifth grade. Moody, hard to get along with, as a senior, Robert finally pushed my last hot button. To the class, I said "Excuse me, but Robert has to go." We walked to the counselor and when she saw him she looked down. She said to me, "No one wants him. He's been kicked out of every class this semester. Yours was a last resort." I went back to class to start the lesson feeling very justified in my release of this very bad young man. My thoughts would not let me concentrate on the lesson, instead a poem by Edwin Markham began to interrupt my thinking.

He drew a circle and shut me out, Heretic, rebel a thing to flout,
But life and I had the wit to win, We drew a circle and took him in.

I listened to my inner feelings, and then shared the poem with the class. "What do you think this means?" I asked the class. One student said, "We've got to bring him back into the group." Can you imagine a stream of 30 young people crowding into the small office to reclaim a classmate? Our forgiveness was wonderful and helped Robert to grow.

FORGIVING TOO QUICKLY

If forgiveness is the essence of working back to equality, one item needs to be brought to the table. Can you forgive too quickly? Forgiveness must include setting new boundaries.

How do we know? The evidence is there: the poor behavior reappears. Some people will use you like a napkin. When behavior is push and take, forgiveness is not the answer. Tough love is! Tough love is the ability to deny the person you love what you know they want, because denial is the only thing that will make them strong.

Even though you ache to take care of them, you shouldn't rescue them. Life will teach, when given the opportunity. Rescue them no more, allow them to fail. Later, both sides can forgive.

"He who cannot forgive breaks
the bridge over which
he must pass himself,
for every man has need
to be forgiven."

DECIDING TO NEVER FORGIVE

Sometimes people make decisions never to forgive. A cousin, aloof and distant during his mother's life, was intolerant of her drinking. My sister and I never experienced anything connected to an alcohol problem with our Aunt Maude. It was hard for him to hold on to the belief of alcoholism when we finally confronted him. He acknowledged that if he judged his friends as harshly as he judged his mother, he would have not have any friends. A year after her death, I asked. "Have you forgiven yourself for ignoring your mother?" He said, "No, would you value me if I forgave myself quickly?"

THE IMPORTANCE OF FORGIVENESS

Forgiveness is essential part of our well-being. Unforgiveness carries a peril to ourselves: the loss of the ability to laugh, and to have perspective a new direction in life. "He who cannot forgive breaks the bridge over which he must pass himself, for every man has need to be forgiven," says George Herbert.

Forgiving something horrible is a complicated matter especially if one has been hurt by someone especially trusted. People who don't forgive, they eventually pollute themselves by damaging relationships with those people around them. In avoiding forgiveness, we also remove any joy in our life. One woman, in losing her son to murder, said of his murderer, "No, I won't forgive him. I can't forgive someone who consciously took something precious from me and I don't think I should." Suzanne and Sidney Simon say in their book, Forgiveness, "Forgiveness is not forgetting, condoning, absolution, self sacrifice or a clear-cut, one time decision. It has many stages of letting go: denial, self-blame, victimizing, indignation, survival and integration."

FORGIVENESS: DENIAL STAGE

"Denial is an attempt to play down the impact or importance of painful past experiences and bury our thoughts and feelings about those experiences." According to the Simons', "**Forgiveness is a process for healing. It is letting go and moving on. It's a need to heal this piece of hurt from my life. Forgiveness is what happens naturally as a result if confronting painful past experiences and healing old wounds,**" says Suzanne. It's what we do with the hurt that makes the difference.

FORGIVENESS STAGES

DENIAL

SELF BLAME

VICTIM

INDIGNATION

SURVIVOR

INTEGRATION

In the denial stage, people pretend that everything is fine when it isn't. The Simons' state "It includes it never happened, or it didn't affect me, or it happened a long time ago, or it wasn't that bad" all are part of the justification of denial. Leaving the denial state involves acknowledging you have been hurt, you still feel the pain, but now you can talk about experiences, and no longer have to push down or ignore past feelings.

FORGIVENESS: SELF BLAME STAGE

"Self blame tries to explain what happened to us by assuming we were somehow responsible for the injuries and injustices we suffered." It can be categorized by the words: if only. "We would not have been hurt <u>if only</u> we had been different and had done things differently. If only I had done or had not done something," state the Simons.

FORGIVENESS: VICTIM STAGE

Unless people decide to break the cycle, they will repeat the offenses given to them. "The victim stage is the most painful and self-destructive, however, being in the victim stage, they do not deny, nor blame themselves. They have intense feelings of helplessness and hopelessness. They can and do name their perpetrator, over and over," state the Simons.

"There are three different victims," according to the Simons, "**the whiner, meaner, and self indulger**." Each uses a particular mind frame and behavior. The whiner has a poor me, martyr, or self pitying attitude who moans and wants others to join him in his pity parties. The meaner has been so hurt they take it out on others; therefore the behavior is that of a batterer, racist, or a person who delights in putting down others. The third kind of victim is the self indulger, who abuses food, alcohol, drugs or money.

FORGIVENESS: INDIGNATION STAGE

"Indignation helps us get in touch with the anger that our painful past experiences generated. Getting in touch with and working through anger is an essential step in the healing process," declare the Simons. It's the desire to be a well and happy person that can finally lead to the survivor stage. People enter into retribution, scheming revenge and eventually poison themselves.

LIFE IS SHORT,

TIME IS FLEETING

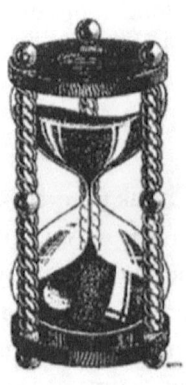

FORGIVE AND MOVE ON!

FORGIVENESS: SURVIVOR STAGE

"In the survivor stage," according to the Simons, "you can realize you have make it though an ordeal. An overall wellness program continues as you become aware of your strengths." Joy, finding your sense of humor, compassion, and helping others like yourself becomes important. Virginia Satir states, "If you have unfinished business about childhood, the message is: Forgiveness is more complete when you allow your parents and yourself into the human race."

Forgiveness allows you to recognize the gifts that only you can give the world. Life is short, time is fleeting, getting yourself motivated to continue your life is the better road to take. Life is tough enough without the baggage of unforgiveness. We all need to forgive to survive in this world. Life is unkind and unfair, but we must recognize our worth and get about the business of making the most of it.

FORGIVENESS: THE INTEGRATION STAGE

"The integration stage acknowledges people who hurt us were doing the best they could do," state the Simons. My first recognition that I hid my angry feelings came from deciding to correct my nail biting behavior some years ago. Through hypnosis, I remembered an eccentric relative, Uncle Nelt, who refused to give me a package, even though it was addressed to my dad, he knew it was for me. He said to my mother "it's against the US Federal law to open anyone's else's mail." When I saw my mother couldn't make Uncle Nelt respond to me as a seven year old I knew I couldn't, so in anger I bit my nails to control my rage.

As an adult, I had to question my unresolved anger: I had only to think of Uncle Nelt when the anger boiled up inside of me. Now dead and gone, he had a personality least like mine, was analytical, lived by the rules, was egocentric, and really thought he was helpful. But as a child, I held on to my frustration a long time. "What am I going to do about it?" The answer was simply: "Let go." That was a big one for me!

Everyone can be our teacher. As I write this, I realized Uncle Nelt was one of my best teachers. Because of this experience, even though I didn't connect it to the hiding anger or my nail biting. I recognized *the desire to be sensitive to children's needs*, to be aware of the harm of always being right, to see another's point of view, and to realize our behavior affects others. I learned a lot very early in life! Did you have a similar experience where you need to forgive some past person and therefore move on with your life?

Overcoming
RELATIONSHIP
DIFFERENCES
CREATES

JOY

ACCOMPLISHMENT

BONDING

PRIDE

MY MOST POTENT TEACHER

My most potent teacher for improving self esteem was Jackie, a victim of child abuse. I was her adult friend, the listening teacher who for years was there when she first came through stages of denial, self blame, victim, indignation, and survivor and integration, I observed her processing the stages of forgiveness. I bear witness to her growth. Jackie mastered the stages of forgiveness and is making a positive difference in this world. Jackie's life emphasizes taking the risk to make positive change.

THE ART OF FRIENDLY CONFRONTATION

Somewhere from my life experience a phrase kept haunting me concerning art: "if all the elements of art are in a photograph or painting, then it become compelling." A photograph that includes all the elements of art: line, designs, shape, repetition, balance, texture, and perspective becomes very interesting.

Likewise, when music touches your heart, the instruments are fine-tuned to each other. After practicing pieces orchestras can produce a masterful rendition of a particular score. It speaks to you and your spirit soars.

Beautiful relationships have elements of both art and music. When people work together using their own unique potential, they produce masterful, beautiful projects even after having a major difference of opinion. People overcoming those differences have a sense of joy, accomplishment, bonding, and pride because they bridged the barriers once thought insurmountable. Because no one sees something exactly like as we see it, **when we use the connecting power of love and the equalizing power of forgiveness, conflict simply becomes part of the harmony**.

Bibliography

Adler, Ron., Towne, Neil, Looking Out/Looking In, Ca: Rinehart Press, 1975

Augsburger, David, When Caring is Not Enough, CA: Herald Press, 1983

Augsburger, David, Caring Enough to Confront, CA: Herald Press, 1983

Bach, George R., Goldberg Herb, Creative Aggression, NT: Doubleday, 1974

Bach, George R., Wyden, Peter, The Intimate Enemy, NT: Avon, 1968

Baer, Jean, How to be an Assertive Women, NY: Signet Books. 1976

Barrett, Nancy, How to Complain and Make it Count, LBJ, Oct 1987

Battle, Melody, Beyond Codependancy, MN, Hazelden Foundation, 1989 Tape

Berne, Eric, Games People Play, CA: Grove Press, 1964

Bendix, Richard, Max Weber, An Intellectual Portrait: 1962

Blake, Robert, Mouton, Jane, The Managerial Grid, TX: Gulf Publishing, 1964

Bramson, Robert, Coping With Difficult People, NY: Dell Publishing, 1981

Brothers, Dr. Joyce, The Brothers System for Liberated Love and Marriage, NY: Avon Books, 1972

Blumstein, Phillip, Ph. D, Schwartz, Pepper, Ph. D. American Couples, NY: Pocket Books, 1985

Carnegie, Dale, How to Win Friends and Influence People, NY: Simon and Schuster, 1964

Clary, Thomas, The Art of War, MA: Shambhola Publications, 1989

Covey, Stephen R, The 7 Habits of Highly Effective People, NY: Simon and Schuster, 1990

Cohey, Herb, You Can Negotiate Anything, NY: Bantam Books, 1980

Douglass, Merrill, The Douglass Company, Grandville, MI 1984

Dunn, David, Try Giving Yourself Away, NY: Prentice Hall, Inc. 1946

Goble, Frank, The Third Force, NY: Washington Square Press, 1977

Fettig, Art, Love is The Target, MI: Growth Unlimited Inc. 1992

Fromme, Allen, The Ability to Love, NY: Farrar, Strass and Girous, 1963

Gordon, Thomas, Parent Effectiveness Training, NY: Peter H Wyden, 1970

Gordon, Thomas, Teacher Effectiveness Training, NY: Peter H Wyden, 1974

Gottlieb, Annie, He Should Know How I Feel, McCalls, Aug 1984

Halpern, Howard W., <u>How to Break Your Addiction to a Person</u>, NY: McGraw, 1983

Harris, Thomas A., <u>I'm Okay—Your Okay</u>, NY: Harper and Row, 1969

Henningsen, Catherine A. <u>Fighting Words</u>, LBJ, Feb. 1992

Jampolsky, Gerald G. <u>Teach Only Love</u>, NY: Bantam Books, 1983

Kennedy, Mopsy Stange, <u>Anger in the Office</u>, Savvy: Aug 1981

Kosssorla, Irene, <u>Go for It! How To Win At Love, Work, and</u>
<u>Play</u>, NY: Delcorte Press

Kostis, Peter<u>, Analytical Driver, Expressive, Amibale: Which One is the Real You</u>?" Golf Digest, Sept 1984

Lahaya, Beverly, <u>How To Develop Your Child's Temperament,</u> OR: Harvest House Publishers, 1977

LaHaye, Tim, Phillips, Bob, <u>Anger is A Choice</u>, MI: Zondervan, 1982

Lauer, Jeanette, & Robert, <u>How Fighting Can Help a Marriage</u>, LHJ, July 1987

Littauer, Florence, <u>Your Personality Tree</u>, TX: Word Books, 1986

Nagler, William Ph. D., <u>The Dirty Half Dozen: Six Radical Rules to Make Relationship Last</u>, The Detroit New, 1992

Newman, Mildred, Berkowitz, Bernard, <u>How To Take Charge of Your Life: Give Till It Hurts</u>, LHJ, March, 1986

Mandino, Og. <u>The Greatest Salesman in the Wo</u>rld, NY: Bantam Books, 1968

Neurenberg, Jesse S., <u>Getting Through To People</u>, NY: Prentice Hall, 1963

Norman Sally, <u>When You Hit the Boiling Point</u>, MI: The Detroit News, Jan 28, 1993

Peck, M Scott M.D., <u>The Road Less Traveled</u>, NY: Touchstone Books, 1978

Perls, Fritz, <u>Gestalt Therapy Verbatim</u>, CA: Real People Press, 1969

Powell, John, <u>The Secret of Staying in Love</u>, IL: Argus Communications, 1974

Powell, John, <u>Why Am I Afraid To Tell You Who I Am?</u>, IL: Argus Communications, 1972

Richter, John W., <u>Caring is, Sharing it</u>, IL: Success Unlimited, March, 1981

Rubin, Theodore, Isaac, <u>The Angry Book</u>, NY: MacMillian, 1969

Ruben, Harvey L., <u>Competing</u>, NY: Pinnacle Books, Inc, 1981

Steiner, Claude, *Scripts People Live*, NY: Grove Press, 1974

Schimel John L, <u>If Fighting Families Didn't Bicker, What Would They Say</u>? Detroit Free Press, June 15, 1980

Schmidt, Kramen, Schmalenberg, <u>Principles of a Productive Conflict Resolution</u>, NY: Contemporary Publishing, 1977

Sheehy, Gail, <u>Passages</u>, NY: Bantam Books, 1977

Sheehy, Gail, <u>Pathfinders</u>, NY: William Morrow, 1977

Shostum, Everett L, <u>Man, The Manipulator</u>, TN, Abington Press, 1967

Simon, Sidney and Suzanne, <u>Forgiveness: How to Make Peace with your Past and Get on With Your Life</u>, Warner Books, 1990

Smith, Donald, <u>The Healing Touch of Attention</u>, NY: Guideposts Asso. 1969

Smith, Hyrum, <u>Gaining Control</u>, UT: Franklin Intn Inst. Inc. 1990, Tape

Strang, Ruth, <u>Adolescent Views Himself</u>, NY: McGraw, 1957

Synowiec, Bertie Ryan, <u>Does Anyone Hear Our Cries for Help?</u> Positive Thinking Seminars, Grosse Ile, MI: 1992

Taffel, Ron, <u>Haven't We Had This Fight Before?</u> McCalls: Dec 1991

Thayer, Stephen, <u>Encounters</u>, Psychology Today, March 1988

Visual, Nemp.otago ac.nz/PDF/writing_98

Walch J. Watson, <u>Conflict and Aggression</u>, MA: Walch Publishers, 1978

Waller, Williard, <u>The Rating and Dating Complex</u>, American Sociological Review, 1937

Wanderer, Dr Sev & Cabot, Tracy, <u>Letting Go</u>, NY: Warner Books, 1978

Waitley, Denis, <u>Being The Best</u>, Nightingale-Conant Corp, Tape

Williams, Redford B., <u>Anger Kills 17 Strategies</u>, NY: Random House, 1993

Williams, Margery, <u>The Velveteen Rabbit</u>, NY: Doubleday, 1980

_____, <u>Battered Women, Why Do They Stay</u>? Psychology Today, May 1992

CLASSROOM ACTIVITIES

CONFRONTATION SKILLS QUIZ

1. What is the purpose of confrontation skills?

2. Name three of the good listening practices in confrontation.

3. What are three of the effective confrontations strategies?

4. What are "I" messages:

   I feel _____ when I see _____ and it makes me
   _____.

5. Name the 3 precursors of conflict.

6. Name the roles involved in the principles of conflict.

7. Name the six forgiveness stages according to Suzanne Simons in her book
   Forgiveness: How to Make Peace with your Past and Get on With Your Life

Answers: 1) Conflict is necessary for needs to be met. 2) Behavior triggers behavior, both positively and negatively. Behavior can be categorized into four different patterns. Understanding behavior patterns helps you adjust. Unmet needs can trigger conflict. Know your own behavior pattern. 3) Leveling, timing, appointments, place, focus, ownership 4) sad, this mess and very upset. 5) Ego, power, control 6) Topdog/underdog 7) Denial, self blame, victim, indignation, survivor and integration.

NAME _____ DATE _____

HOW DO PEOPLE HANDLE CONFRONTATION?

Review role playing for understanding conflict about husbands and wives.
Students use paper to mark behaviors as role plays progress.

The dialogue is the opening line, the mate simple responds.

SCENE I   **Wife is lonesome, interrupts TV baseball game that husband is watching.**

- Dear, I hate to bother you, but I was looking forward to spending today together.
- You give that TV set more attention than you give to me.
- Turn off that blasted idiot box and listen to me for once.

SCENE II   **Husband finds bill where wife has charged $200 on Visa.**

- You did it again, what did you buy this time?
- You stupid _____, do you think money grows on trees?
- I got the bill from Visa, dear.

SCENE III   **Husband start to track through wet mopped floor.**

- What's wrong with your eyes, can't you see the floor is wet?
- Honey, can you wait or go around to the other door?
- How would you like to mop this floor yourself?

SCENE IV   **Wife forgets to pick up suit at the cleaners in time for a wedding.**

- How would you feel if I forgot your best dress at the cleaners?
- You mean to tell me that I've got to wear that blue suit?
- That does it. I just won't go. I didn't want to go anyway.

Shirley Brackett Mathey

Scoring: Make check marks or notes for volunteers.

Couple 1   Couple 2   Couple 3   Couple 4

Who:

Was the person in the top dog role?

Changed the subject

Understood other person's point of view.

Used humor well.

Admitted mistakes

Caved in too early

Apologized inappropriately

Identified the specific area of disagreement.

Tried to work things out.

Wanted to decide who was right.

Pretended to agree.

Threatened the person.

Whined or complained until they got their way.

Wanted both people happy with the decision.

Talked when they should have listened.

Made it easy for others to agree with them.

NAME _____ DATE _____

SELF ESTEEM
DEALING WITH CONFLICT
SITUATIONS

Circle the rating most like you to recognize
elements of self esteem and conflict.

ARE YOU FOOLING YOURSELF

Never   Sometimes   Always

TAKING RESPONSIBILITY FOR OTHERS

Never   Sometimes   Always

KNOWING CONSEQUENCES OF YOUR BEHAVIOR

Never   Sometimes   Always

WHAT DOES KEEPING THE PEACE MEAN TO YOU

Never   Sometimes   Always

RESPONDING TO PEER PRESSURE

Never   Sometimes   Always

ACCEPTABLE FEELINGS ABOUT AUTHORITY

Never   Sometimes   Always

IMPATIENCE WITH OTHERS

Never   Sometimes   Always

THINKING BEFORE YOU SPEAK

Never   Sometimes   Always

LOOKING BEFORE YOU LEAP

Never   Sometimes   Always

ACTING BECAUSE YOU CARE

Never   Sometimes   Always

NAME _____ DATE _____

www.ingramcontent.com/pod-product-compliance
Lightning Source LLC
Chambersburg PA
CBHW020249290526
45784CB00003B/1161